Praise for *Good*

"This rare and revelatory gem offers ﹍﹍﹍﹍﹍﹍﹍﹍
to restore innermost connection with yourself, the earth and all that lives on
her. This book is a powerful invitation to open your heart to healing wisdom
teachings from within and demands to be read again and again."

—**PRAJNAPARAMITA**, author *Wings of Freedom*, founder of La Roserie de Sacha

"As a psychiatrist, psychotherapist, psychosomatic doctor and also a neurologist
and neuroscientist, it's my daily business to treat and heal people going
through the deep night of the soul. Tanis' new book is a light in the night
and an important guide on the journey, to contact the wisdom, experience
and wellness of the body for deeper healing and transformation of illness.
This important book supports all the people to whom a new medicine, and
understanding of the human body and of healing power is important.
Good Morning Henry is a guide on this path."

—**CHRISTIAN SCHOPPER, MD/MHBA**, neurology, psychiatry,
psychotherapy, medicine VAOAS Zurich and lecturer University of Zurich

"Soooo brilliant! Good Morning Henry is an endless source of extraordinary
perceptions of the multi-level reality of human life. Tanis Helliwell's writing style
is so dynamic, captivating, clear and yet abounds with humour and joy as her
conversations with Henry help the reader to reflect and contemplate his or her life."

—**MARIELLE CROFT**, astrologer and teacher

"I think your style is quite unique – no matter how much of a
'homemade' simplistic and populist spin you put on your work, your
intelligent, searching questions mean you let nothing escape and
you excavate every nook and cranny. I think your nimble and high
intelligence is why you were meant to write this book."

—**STEPHEN ROBERTS**

"Good Morning Henry shows us how to turn within, how to ask for answers and
how to listen for the deep knowledge and strength that's been waiting patiently
inside us all….I will be re-reading the book several times as there is so much to learn
from it and applying the guidelines to help myself take back my latent power."

—**HEATHER SIMPKIN**, Playwright, Producer, Bear in the Air Productions

Good Morning Henry

AN IN-DEPTH JOURNEY
WITH THE BODY INTELLIGENCE

TANIS HELLIWELL
foreword by RICHARD RUDD

Published by Wayshower Enterprises

Library and Archives Canada Cataloguing in Publication

Good Morning Henry: an in-depth journey with the body intelligence
by Tanis Helliwell.

Includes bibliographical references and index.

ISBN 978-1-987831-32-0 (Lightning Source)

Spirituality | Healing | Self-actualization (Psychology) | Peace of mind

CC BL624 .H45 2022 | DDC 204/.4—dc23

Cover and interior design by Melany Hallam, Maywood Design

Published by Wayshower Enterprises

https://www.tanishelliwell.com
https://www.myspiritualtransformation.com

DEDICATION

With gratitude to Paramahansa Yogananda and all masters for the assistance they give us in awakening to our destiny.

CONTENTS

FOREWORD

I first met Tanis Helliwell five years ago when she came to visit me at my home in Devon, England. As soon as I met her I sensed that she was a magical person, a person with great natural wisdom and a unique perception of many dimensions of understanding. I am a great proponent of the art of 'magical thinking', and Tanis has this gift in spades. Magical thinking is the ability to actively use the creative imagination alongside one's intuition to unlock life's secrets. However, I know many people who can think magically, but are they all wise? I am not so sure. So often when we set off on a journey to explore the great perennial wisdom, we never get beyond the realm of fantasy. The shelves of the average new age book shop are filled with such books.

This book, *Good Morning Henry*, is different. It does contain a great deal of magical thinking, but it is also clearly written by someone who has truly experienced suffering and who has transcended many layers and levels of reality. *Good Morning Henry* has the feeling of a direct spiritual transmission, but it is written in such a down-to-earth way that you almost don't even notice the streams of wisdom you are imbibing as you pass through its pages.

It takes time for wisdom to mature and ripen in a human soul. This book is filled with insights that have been garnered over years and years of seeking, inquiring and waiting patiently for things to make sense. The book also covers a vast territory. It is not a book that could have been written by an ordinary person. This is the work of an ancient time-traveler—a magician who understands the fractal nature of reality and who is at home within the labyrinth of the timeless truth.

Of course, there is also a thread of lovely 'leprechaunian' humour running throughout the text, and this lightness helps the reader to relax and enjoy the wonderful ride Tanis takes us on. *Good Morning Henry* is filled not just with mind-bending concepts, but also harmonizes with scientific insight and practical truth. This is not just inspiring but is also a highly useful book, rooted in the body, the earth and in everyday life.

Wherever you are in your spiritual journey, *Good Morning Henry* will help you to take the next step. Take a deep breath therefore, clear your mind, open your heart and let the magic carry you along the river of words within ...

—RICHARD RUDD

INTRODUCTION

Re-examine all you have been told, dismiss what insults your soul, and your very flesh will become a great poem.

WALT WHITMAN

We are in a time of great change. Although we might like to think that the world will return to safety and the old 'normal' shortly, I propose it is not to be. You may think me a pessimist and doomsayer. On the contrary, I'm optimistic and hopeful that we are entering a new dawn when we will re-establish our connection with natural and universal laws to discover our true destiny.

There is a term associated with this great transition that we are undergoing collectively—the dark night of the soul. This dark night is created by the unstable world situation with collapse of environmental, economic, social and health structures which we believed were a secure foundation. And now dark nights are happening not only to people in mid-life but even to children and those in their teens and 20s. These young people see no hope in life because of the dark cloud of global collapse hanging over them.

During a dark night, and what may appear at the time to be a calamity, the anchors of our life are ripped away and we find ourselves adrift in a world lacking meaning or safety. To come out on the other side we need a new set of values, which are life-sustaining and based on love and health of all beings. These new values transcend the ego-based state that has dominated our world until now. Universal consciousness sets up each of us to succeed, not fail, in life's challenges but that doesn't mean it will be easy. However, the more we embrace the dark night as a great gift in all its manifestations the quicker and more easily it leads to fulfilling our individual and collective human destiny.

Alchemy, on deeper levels, is a metaphysical process to transmute our baser nature into the gold of self-realization and we are being called now to become alchemists. This time arises when we are tired of suffering and are ready to journey to our core and to commit to changing ourselves from the inside out. Within the dark night the golden nugget awaits that, when found, catapults us to freedom and the light.

And when is a good time to embark on this journey? Any time is a good time. But sometimes the universe gives us a little nudge. This time is now. Our world is in a great PAUSE. Around the world individuals are being strongly encouraged to review their priorities and values and to take the deep dive into their inner selves to discover anew a meaning to sustain their lives in beauty and with alignment to physical, emotional and spiritual well-being.

This is not a journey for sissies! You might start the journey willingly or be conscripted through life's circumstances but regardless you will be confronting your shadow, the dark and even unknown parts of yourself that you have disregarded and denied. But the gold nugget where your true power resides is found in this dark. And just to be clear, this journey is also one of joy. There are glorious breakthroughs of knowing and 'ahas' where pieces of the puzzle you have constructed in your life fall into place and deeper levels of truth, compassion and heart-opening for yourself and others occur as if spontaneously by themselves. You learn as you journey to be gentle with yourself and, as you do this, the path forward moves more easily and you discover that you're supported by benevolent forces beyond your control or human understanding.

Each of us has been given the best possible gift to help us find our gold. That is free will. By activating and aligning your will to universal principles, you can control your destiny and create your reality. To be sure, each of us has an inherited physical, emotional, mental and spiritual blueprint to work with. However, you and I are absolutely PERFECT to achieve our life's purpose and to fulfill our soul's, not our ego's, plans for us. The effects of our daily choices transcend this life. Therefore, procrastination and putting things off for tomorrow is not a positive option as delay only increases long-term suffering.

That last point may seem harsh and hard to take until you realize that you receive help every step along the way. You are never alone. Your higher self, your soul, and its alignment with universal consciousness closes doors that lead away from your highest good and gives you firm nudges when you veer off course. These nudges often come as health, environmental, relationship, financial and work crises saying, "Stop!" And just as often doors open to better opportunities and discoveries in these same areas saying, "Go this way!"

And how do your soul and universal consciousness produce these monumental changes in your life? To answer this question, I would like to introduce you to the precious helper, the consciousness, inside you. Eckhart Tolle refers to this consciousness as the inner body; Rudolph Steiner calls it the body elemental. I often think of it as the body spirit or etheric body because universal intelligence within ether, or space, directs the plan to build your physical, emotional and mental bodies. You may think of it as your conscience or the small inner voice within you.

Whatever term you choose is unimportant just as long as you learn to communicate with this body intelligence because it's an expert in mining and locating the best areas to discover your gold. My mining expert is called Henry and he has helped me to write this guide for committed miners who are seeking a heart of gold.

Good Morning Henry explores the importance of developing a harmonious relationship with your body intelligence and how to accomplish this. Connecting with this body consciousness reconnects you to natural laws which are the same as spiritual laws. It's the quickest, most direct way that I know to transform from an ego-centered to consciousness-centered being which is our next stage in evolution. As Eckhart Tolle says, "The fact is that no one has ever become enlightened through denying or fighting the body…In the end you will always have to return to the body, where the essential work of transformation takes place. Transformation is through the body, not away from it."[1]

Learning about the importance of the consciousness in the body has been an evolving process for me as I uncover deeper and deeper layers of its life-giving importance. From this process, I've learned why we have illness, disease and weakness in our body and mind and how to work with the body intelligence to heal them. And this consciousness wants to work with you to gain abundant health.

---

1   Eckhart Tolle, *The Power of Now* (Vancouver: Namaste Publishing, 1999) p. 114

Your body intelligence—being an expert gold miner—can guide you into the dark pit where your unconscious thoughts are stored and bring these thoughts to consciousness where you can heal them. By doing this, you can discover your life scripts and the negative thoughts that sabotage you. You can uncover the fears that are limiting you and their underlying cause. You can learn of the family and cultural conditioning that undermines you from fulfilling your destiny. Then, working consciously with your body intelligence, you're able to transmute the ancestral wounds and traumas through your biological lineage, both backward and forward in time to find the gold nuggets within.

You may ask, "How does this alchemical transformation occur?" When you eliminate the illusions that you operate under, you develop your love, wisdom and will, along with other positive qualities, that raise your frequency granting you both consciousness and transforming energy. These qualities develop naturally as you embrace the golden gifts discovered during your dark night of the soul and the consciousness in your body sheds light on your dark places as it accompanies you through this process. This alchemical process promotes brain and heart synching that transform you at a cellular level to heal your body.

Furthermore, your personal healing and transformation have a direct impact on transforming these same patterns in the collective unconscious of humanity. This is not just nice to do, it is essential in order to awaken to your human destiny. You can talk to this wise guide—and my hope is that you will—and discover for yourself how it's waiting to help you. This powerful process will strengthen you in any way you need it.

It sounds like a tall order but it isn't. It's the simplest of journeys taking you to your center where your love, joy and power reside.

Mystics have always said, "Your answers lie within you." My hope is that this book is both a testament to this wisdom and an encouragement to dialogue with your body intelligence to realize the truth of this statement for yourself. As such, *Good Morning Henry* can act as a guide for self-transformation.

Good Morning Henry is written in a friendly and unique style as a conversation between my body consciousness and myself. He is the wise one and I the student who is sometimes quite clever and sometimes really needing help. If Henry only covered what is pertinent to me there would be no book. But he chooses topics that are predictable stumbling blocks that most individuals will encounter on their spiritual path. The topics and conversations are offered to you as an example of how you, too, can talk to your wise inner guide.

I first met this wise guide in 1985 while on a spiritual retreat. During a meditation, I was surprised to discover that my body housed another consciousness—one that called itself my body elemental and spoke about its purpose in my life. It said that most humans are ignorant of its existence and that it wanted me to teach others about its importance. Dutifully, I wrote about this body intelligence in two books and felt that I had fulfilled its request, however others kept calling me back to it. Psychiatrists, doctors and many people asked me to teach workshops called *Spiritual-Body Psychotherapy* and *Self-Healing with the Body Elemental* devoted to this topic.

Encouraged by the physical, psychological and spiritual healing that participants encountered in these workshops, as they released layers of trauma and pain, I began writing a book about these techniques. But it felt dry, so I put it away, content to wait forever, if need be, until new inspiration came.

Six years later, while browsing on my computer, my fingers suddenly typed, "Good morning Henry" and I heard an inner voice, which I recognized as my body intelligence, say loud and clear, "Tomorrow we start."

NOTE TO THE READER

Welcome and thanks for joining me on this journey as we explore the art of alchemical gold mining. I'm grateful that you felt called to read *Good Morning Henry* and fully respect your free choice in how quickly or thoroughly you wish to proceed. That said, there are a few tips to hopefully make your journey more enjoyable and profitable.

1. If you are a strong mental, intellectual type who loves tons of data the good news is that it is coming. HOWEVER, I recommend that you don't race through the book in time to race on to the next one. Gold mining is about pausing to reflect on the best vein to explore, the best path to take. Pause to allow the information to seep into your emotions and cells of your physical body. This is how transformation occurs.

2. If you are a strong emotional type, one who eats up self-help books and loves to spend time talking about feelings, you may have a tendency to go down into the mine and stay there indefinitely to find more gold nuggets. Please don't. When you find a gold nugget bring it up to the surface and put your gold into practice in the world.

3. If you are a highly kinesthetic 'prove it to me' 'seeing is believing' kind of person this book might be challenging in another way. Why? Because Spirit, the eternal boundless principle that transcends space and time, isn't provable to the concrete human mind. However, in this book you will find practical solutions in the examples I've used that you will be able to relate to and that will help you in your own life.

"Tanis provides practical steps we can take to reconnect and partner with our body consciousness to move from being ego-centered to soul-centered. Because there is so much knowledge and wisdom packed into each chapter, I highly recommend taking time to contemplate, reflect and absorb the material before moving on to the next chapter. I found myself going back to reread sections and each time I 'got it' at a deeper level."

— Merle Dulmadge, President, ETRA Therapeutic Riding Assoc.

Part 1:

GETTING TO KNOW
WHO RUNS THE SHOW

Do not second-guess spirit;
Your lists of preferences
Mean nothing.
Spirit is not interested in your comfort,
But in breaking you apart
Until your shell crumbles
And you are reborn as love.

TANIS HELLIWELL, *Embraced by Love*

1

THE UNSUNG HERO:
YOUR BODY INTELLIGENCE

Who looks outside dreams; who looks inside awakes.
CARL JUNG, *Letters, Vol. 1*

Morning found me contemplating three half-completed books that were stockpiled seeking birth. None of these involved the body intelligence who I felt was urging me to write about its function in our lives. My stalled attempt to write anything of consequence, some years earlier, probably accounted for my lackluster feelings that morning. Reluctantly, I stood up and walked to the computer and pushed the power key.

Surrendering to the moment, I heard, "You were not ready to hear what I had to say before, but you are now." It was as if the consciousness within my body was responding to my thoughts. We were not separate but One and what he said I already intuitively knew. Since a child, I have been able to glide through the physical, emotional, mental and soul realms in an instant. At the same time, I was able to separate what he said and what I heard into a dialogue that, I'd found in the past, might benefit others as well as myself.

"Of course, I'm listening to your thoughts, much better than you do by the way. Don't be so surprised. Haven't I communicated with you over the years?"

"I've written about what you taught me in two books and I don't know if there is much else to say," I replied.

"Correction! You wrote about me 'briefly' before."

"Why is this important now?" I asked, still not convinced that this was the best use of my time.

"Because the moment is right. There comes a time in the life of all humans, be it in this life or another, when the unconscious must become conscious. In fact, humans cannot evolve further unless this happens. For you, as with most people, this process has been ongoing in dribs and drabs over your entire life, with surges forward every decade or so. This is the most common way that spiritual and psychological seekers uncover their unconscious, but—and it is a big BUT—at some point the merging must take place. What I say will benefit many people who are going through a dark night of the soul and who need this information."

"I don't see how my personal situation will benefit anyone else," I argued, still hoping to keep my conversation with my body intelligence private.

"Let me explain," my body intelligence replied, trying to mollify me. "The world is going through a paradigm shift that will affect all people globally. It's the end of the era of ego and the beginning of the era of the conscious human, and people need help bridging these two realities. It's a difficult time when their reality will be shattered and their ego will struggle to hold onto their old self and world view. Many, if not most, will go through a dark inner time. As the health, government, financial and relationship structures and beliefs they have been attached to crumble, they will undergo a crisis of meaning. They will become depressed, angry, resentful and hopeless and experience 'not knowing' and emptiness as they realize they are not in control of their lives. In fact, of anything."

"Although I can see that this topic is important," I replied, "I don't see why I need to write a book about this. To be honest writing about this topic doesn't seem like fun to me and I'd prefer to have a break from these heavy topics."

"This is your ego, not your soul, speaking and this is about to change," my body consciousness was quick to say. "You might like to think of yourself as unique but everyone's ego is basically the same and uses the same games to control you. In this book I—or should I say we—will discuss the ego's various avoidance tactics and how to remove them as this is the path to freedom and your next stage in evolution. The topics in this book create a bridge for you and others to travel from the ego-centered to self-realized state. This journey—be it short or long, difficult or relatively easy—ultimately leads to freedom and to surrendering to live and love more fully."

My heart fluttered as I contemplated the responsibility for helping others with information that I may not practice myself. "I have always thought that everyone has to go through a dark night of the soul by themselves," I replied, still not ready to acquiesce.

"No need to be anxious," my body intelligence said. "It's true that each person individually goes through the transformation from being ego-centered to soul-centered. Yet, a book or a chat with someone who has gone through the process can give others tips to help.

"Let me give you an analogy. Until now, humans have been like caterpillars eating up their environment. There's nothing wrong with this as this caterpillar stage—that of the ego—is a stage in conscious development. However, universal intelligence is now making it clear that stage has come to an end. It is now time to enter the cocoon stage. There, you are meant to pause and contemplate your life and let go of what no longer serves you or your world knowing that, by doing so, you will find your true destiny.

"On the surface this process may look like death and an end but it is merely a stage towards the birth of a new era in your and humanity's evolution into full creators with universal intelligence. In the cocoon a caterpillar digests itself to turn into a butterfly. The butterfly in many traditions is the symbol for the soul and the awakened human who is united with universal consciousness. The cocoon stage is a difficult time for individuals because they are neither one thing nor another. Their body elemental or body intelligence, if you prefer, wants to help them through this process and together we can show them how to do this. This is an organic process that comes to all humans, like dying."

"Is this meant to reassure me?" I retorted, concerned. "If you're so smart you must know that dying is everyone's greatest fear. I'm sure that everyone would rather skip the cocoon and go straight to the butterfly stage."

I could hear my body intelligence laughing, "Of course you would but that is not how transformation works. And, as I keep mentioning, the body elementals of others can help quicken and ease the dark night process just like I'm helping you. Be assured. We are doing this together and universal consciousness supports this timing. Let's start again, shall we?"

"Very well," I replied, attempting to move into deeper trust and faith, while a hodge-podge of thoughts and feelings ran rampant through me.

I felt at One with consciousness and had no fear, while simultaneously my personality was concerned. By lightly altering my thoughts, I could fully explore all levels of consciousness to better understand how it worked in the physical, emotional and mental bodies and how to free any stuck places. However, perhaps the personality filter, which I used to do this, needed an overhaul. I realized the body intelligence wanted this.

"Perhaps I'd best start with the basics and say more about myself." I felt him/her/it waiting for my agreement.

"Him/her/it is actually an accurate way of thinking about me, but you can call me Henry."

"Stop. Don't rush ahead. I want to know more about the him/her/it bit and how you've come up with 'Henry'?"

"Alright, I'll back up. Think of me as a body elemental or, specifically, your body elemental. I, like everyone's body elemental, have been with you in this life since conception."

Henry spoke slowly and any anxiety I had felt turned to curiosity.

"When the father's sperm and mother's egg merged, I downloaded mainly into the DNA, RNA and other smaller components, yet to be discovered, the pattern that you would work with in your present existence. This pattern is not only physical, such as gender, body type, hair color, but also emotional, mental and spiritual characteristics that you think of as 'me'."

"You call yourself a 'body elemental'. Could you tell me what that term means?" I asked.

"Let's start with the word 'elemental'. Most humans speak of four elements: earth, air, fire and water. I am a being of the fifth element—ether—and I work with the other four elements to build your body. Let me explain what I mean. It's scientifically proven that matter, such as a chair, a plant, even your human body, is mostly ether—space. What I refer to as ether, the New Biophysics refers to as the quantum vacuum. And what you think of as matter is actually more than 99.9 percent ether.

"I am the conscious intelligence that creates form from ether by organizing it into various vibrational frequencies. With the lowest frequencies I create your physical body; with somewhat higher frequencies I create your emotional body; and with even higher frequencies I create your mental body. As an etheric being, I exist in all these frequencies and build physical, emotional and mental forms according to the frequencies of your thoughts."

"The cellular biologist, Bruce Lipton," I interjected, "has written about how the cells of our body are affected by our thoughts and how the new science of epigenetics is revolutionizing our understanding of the link between mind and matter and how our personal and collective lives are affected. So, I am familiar with what you are saying however do you suggest that I and others apply this information to change our lives?"

"I, like all body elementals, work with the karmic blueprint of your physical, emotional, mental and spiritual characteristics to build the personality vessel. Within this code are both your weaknesses and the gifts to overcome them. You have free will to choose minute-to-minute to follow the higher road of heart opening and life-giving thoughts or the lower road of ego control that leads to suffering."

Henry stressed, "It's key for you to know, really know, that your consciousness survives death and what we are referring to as the dark night of the soul is mostly your past karma playing out as you suffer your way to wisdom and joy. You can alter this program because your thoughts, emotions and actions program me as well. Earlier in your evolution you did this unconsciously but, as you evolve, you do this consciously. I want you to think of me as your partner in this alchemical transformational process that turns the lead of your animal nature to the gold of a self-realized human."

"I must say this sounds attractive but what do you mean by my 'karmic' blueprint and who gives it to you?"

"In the ethers are stored the record, which is your karma, of all of your previous lives and what you have the potential to become. There are great beings working with universal consciousness who, along with your spiritual higher Self, oversee your evolution. They decide the patterns to give you in this life to best move you forward to your destiny. So, the karmic blueprint contains the frequencies for all the patterns that you need to evolve in this lifetime. I incorporate the strengths and talents, as well as wounds and weaknesses from past lives, for you to achieve your purpose in this life."

"Could you say more about how you actually put my unique pattern in my physical body?" I asked.

"Not yet," he replied. "That's enough for today. Pause and reflect on what we've discussed. There is no point in grasping intellectually what I am saying. You will never become self-realized by reading more books. Spiritual transformation occurs through allowing the information to catalyze your emotions so you feel the reality of what I say. When you do this, your cells release old programs that limit you and your frequency rises to a higher level. This is how I help you evolve and tomorrow we will continue this discussion."

After Henry withdrew, I reflected on what he had said. I realized he was correct in his assessment of me. I did love learning new things intellectually, especially about how we can apply new biological findings with spiritual insights to positively affect the cells of our body. But did I take enough time to let these ideas digest and allow them to infiltrate my cells? That seemed more like a being practice and I leaned more towards doing. All too often, being seemed more like doing nothing to me, which was an absence of something rather than a gift in itself. Contemplating my prejudice for doing at the expense of being, I felt the importance of Henry's suggestion. This, in turn, encouraged me to take a deep breath, exhale and relax into being.

2

YOU AND YOUR BODY
INTELLIGENCE ARE LIFE PARTNERS

The core you are afraid to enter turns out to be
the source of what you are looking for.
JOSEPH CAMPBELL, *Reflections on the Art of Living*

The next morning, not surprisingly, I had several questions ready to ask Henry. He did not disappoint and was there immediately when I turned my attention towards him.

"Yesterday you broke off our conversation," I began, "just as you were speaking of how you build my physical, emotional and mental bodies. Can you tell me this now?"

"I'm happy to see that you are taking time to pause and integrate what I'm saying," he answered. "This is important to do daily as it will allow the transformational process to work with you at a cellular level."

"Message taken," I replied, attempting to remain patient. "So is it possible that you can speak about how you work with my physical body now?"

"I work with your medulla and pineal gland to imprint these frequencies of who you have been, who you are now, and who you have the potential to become. Humans are still learning about the functioning of the pineal gland."

"We know," I mentioned, happy to share my own knowledge, "that there are photoreceptors within the cells of the pineal gland which appear to tell the pituitary what to do. Traditional western science currently thinks the pituitary is the master gland of the body, but I think it is the pineal. Mystics from many traditions refer to the pineal gland as 'the third eye' and believe that it has a direct link to consciousness."

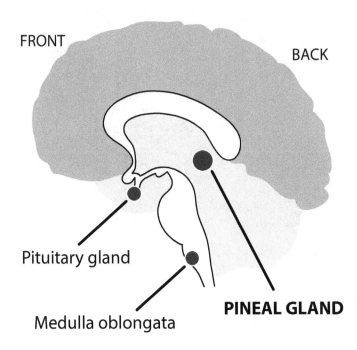

FRONT

BACK

Pituitary gland

Medulla oblongata

PINEAL GLAND

"This is all true," replied Henry patiently. "However, you asked me to explain how 'I' work with the pineal gland, didn't you?"

"Yes," I replied, feeling a little chastised. It was all too easy to show off and cling to what I already recognized rather than open up to hear something new.

"No need to be so hard on yourself. Years ago, you started referring to the pineal as the 'unicell' and as the master gland of the body, and you are partially correct. I download the etheric blueprint embedded in the DNA and other components at conception and place it in the medulla to create the physical, emotional and mental bodies of the individual. The universal life force, sometimes called *prana*, primarily enters the body through the medulla. From here it links with the pineal, which is the center of universal intelligence in the body, to spiritually transform the person.

"The pineal gland is not only a physical but also a spiritual organ that changes depending on the thoughts and feelings you have. When your thoughts and feelings are positive—and there are levels of positive emotions—your frequency rises. This is like a key turning a lock that opens up higher states of consciousness. Of course, the reverse is also true. If you generate negative thoughts and emotions, your frequency lowers and the door to higher states closes. Still, all is not lost. Because you remember being in the higher state, you deeply know that it is possible to achieve it again. Yearning to return to higher consciousness is embedded in the codes of all beings and encourages their evolution. A desire to return to Eden, you might call it."

"Can you please stop for a minute? I have a question," I asserted firmly, trying to check my understanding. "The New Biology says that there is no center of consciousness in the body and that the cells, organs and all components are a self-organized network of interconnected and interpenetrating systems."

"That's true," Henry replied. "I am the conscious intelligence within all these."

"Then how can we speak about the function of the DNA or pineal gland?" I asked confused.

"If we're speaking about the physical organ," he answered, "there is one level of reality. If we refer to more subtle levels, there is a deeper reality. Both realities are accurate. There is not one truth within the world of form, truth evolves as your understanding does."

Encouraged by Henry's information about the human body, I asked, "Do animals and trees, for example, also have a body elemental and is it the same as a body intelligence?"

"Body elementals build the physical, emotional and mental bodies of all beings while they exist in the world of form. In fact, the 'human body' you refer to has microRNA that is found in plants and animals that go back to your earliest evolution. You contain this microRNA within you."

"I'm curious about when your work with me ends and what happens meantime? And, while you're at it, do you want to be called a body intelligence or body elemental?"

"When beings evolve past the higher form realms," Henry replied, "they no longer need a body elemental. And regarding your second question that you managed to slip in, whether you call me a body elemental, body intelligence or body consciousness is immaterial, it's understanding my function that is important."

I could see by his reply that I wouldn't be able to slip anything past him unnoticed but I felt that he was entirely tolerant of my quirks and so I might as well indulge my curiosity.

"Many great masters, such as Jesus, Babaji and Sri Yukteswar," I said, "are able to re-create a physical body after death. They can move in space and time and appear in a physical form to many people. Is this because they are working consciously with their body elementals?"

"Absolutely," Henry replied. "And this is what all humans will do when they reach a certain level of consciousness, but this happens in stages. Right now, you and others have to focus on the stage you are in. I, like their body elementals, control instinctive bodily functions, such as breathing, heartbeat, sleeping, orgasm and hunger. To evolve and, for perfect health, you must learn to control these systems consciously and regulate the amounts of air, water, fire and earth elements in your body. I can help you to do this."

"Doing these things seems impossible to me presently and I'm sure others would feel the same," I said, overwhelmed by what he was suggesting. It was one thing to speak theoretically and another to put his recommendations into practice.

"It is possible or I wouldn't suggest it. I AM you. We are not separate. Many Atlanteans worked consciously with their body elementals and did these things. Some could also levitate, bring rain, light fires with the mind, practice telepathy and clairvoyance, demanifest and manifest their bodies at will, and travel in time and space. These qualities were lost through the growing dominance of the ego which wants to control you. Now this is changing as humans begin to move beyond the control of the ego."

"I can believe you intellectually but that doesn't mean I can do it. This is very frustrating and depressing. Maybe, if you make it simple, I'll be able to release the energy that is stuck in my physical body. That's what you want, isn't it?"

"Even having that thought transforms your consciousness and begins to accomplish your goal to remove control from your ego to align with universal intelligence," Henry replied.

"That's hopeful," I countered, now relieved, before asking, "Please explain how my thoughts hasten or retard my transformation?"

"Okay. Let's look at fear. Fears hold you back from accomplishing your goals if you let them control you. But you can change them by using your will to change your thoughts from negative to positive and from fear to love. Doing this lessens the control of the ego which, in turn, raises your frequency until you release the last vestiges of fear-based patterns and become conscious, without an ego."

"So, are you saying that my willingness to step forward and try what you recommend, even if I fear failing, reduces ego control?"

"That's it exactly," Henry answered. "And the stronger you trust that you will succeed, the quicker this works."

"Do my or other's thoughts override the original program which body intelligences use to construct our personality vessels?"

"We program what you unconsciously and consciously give us. Simply put, negative thoughts strengthen the ego and positive thoughts weaken it, as positive thoughts are more aligned to universal intelligence. The more your thoughts are in harmony with universal intelligence the less control the ego has and the faster you move out of the dark night and emerge into the light of consciousness."

"Could you say more about how you program us?" I wanted to make sure I was leaving no stone unturned.

"Humans have free will and learn over time to move from being unconscious to being conscious. When individuals are not conscious, their body elementals use both their individual karmic program plus the collective memory of their species to build their bodies. This collective memory, called by Carl Jung the 'collective unconscious', includes not only that of humans but also of all beings on Earth. We anchor this entire etheric program in the physical body mainly through the DNA and RNA."

My eyes must have gone blank for Henry continued, "Am I confusing you? I'll explain.

"Humans are strange. They love to think that their feelings and thoughts are unique. This is erroneous. Let's examine fears again in more detail. All fears, like feeling unloved, rejected, unworthy and guilty, are part of the collective archetypes of all humans, as are fears of failing, the unknown, change, loss of control. And the fears of humans are exactly opposite to their hopes and dreams of being loved, successful, accepted, happy, safe. You get the picture.

"This means—and be patient as I feel you chomping at the bit to ask a question—that humans inherit at conception both a unique combination of qualities to fulfill their destiny, as well as collective archetypes of all humanity and of all living beings. As you and others achieve your destiny, you assist the collective human archetypes to evolve, as well as contributing your gifts to the evolution of the Earth and all its species. This law is true both for humans and all species. The reverse is also true. If beings do not succeed in their life purpose, their failure sets back the evolution of their species."

"I get it," I replied. "I have always believed that each of us is set up to succeed and not to fail in achieving whatever our purpose is."

"That is correct. Why would universal intelligence set you up to fail?"

"Easy to say but, when your life takes a downturn, it's sometimes difficult to believe that the universe is on your side," I interrupted.

"True," Henry granted. "Still, the destiny of humanity is to evolve to become conscious creators. That means using their free will to choose their behavior, which entails ups and downs in their evolutionary path, with more ups as individuals become increasingly conscious."

"Let's get back to you," I requested. "Please say more about how body elementals evolve."

"Our relationship is complicated," Henry teased my curiosity. "Even as you have evolved through thousands of lifetimes, so have I. We have been together since the beginning, when you first separated from the universal intelligence, sometimes called the Creator. Until that time, you had no need of a being devoted to creating and sustaining your body, because you were a spiritual being without form in complete union with universal love.

"When you separated from the source of consciousness—and this is the story for all humans—you descended into form. This took place over millennia. You became an individual who believed you needed a vessel to contain your single identity. At that time, you brought me into form by impressing your thoughts on the ethers that, in turn, gradually descended into the elements that compose physical matter. In the Bible, this is when Adam and Eve saw they were naked, felt ashamed, and left Eden—which was the state of living in complete oneness with universal intelligence.

"Originally, I was like clothes to protect you from harsher and harsher emotional and physical environments as you descended further into form and fell from the conscious into the unconscious state. As you descended, you continued to program me by your thoughts and feelings, but you were no longer aware of what you were doing. Over lifetimes, I started to recognize repetitive patterns of positive or negative thoughts and gradually became aware of the likely result—be it pleasure or pain—from them."

"Did your recognition coincide with me becoming consciously aware of these same patterns?"

"Indeed, they did. As you become increasingly conscious, so do I."

"Therefore, your evolution is tied directly to mine," I concluded.

Another thought presented itself. "When I become self-realized, like the butterfly you mentioned yesterday, what happens to you? You said that I originally brought you into form, so will you dissolve like the ego?"

"An excellent question." Henry paused to consider before answering. "When you no longer need a physical, emotional or mental vessel, the vessel dissolves at which time I'm freed to reunite with the whole."

"How do you know that?" I asked.

"Not such a leap. In between your incarnations, I return to the group soul of body elementals, those who build bodies for all humans. This happens after I download into the Book of Life, otherwise called the Akashic Records, the knowledge of all that occurred during your preceding lifetime. The Akashic Records holds the collective memory for all humans and beings evolving on Earth. Then, when it is time for you to reincarnate, I build the vessel for your next life by using the necessary information from these records. But…when you no longer need to reincarnate, neither do I."

"Absolutely great for both of us. When you are united with your group soul of body elementals between incarnations, do you continue to evolve?"

"Think of body elementals as body spirits. Because we are spirit beings, we don't sleep like humans do and, when you are incarnated, we're on duty 24/7 during both waking and sleeping states. We evolve when we maintain the bodies of our individual hosts. When we have time off between your incarnations, we are united with universal intelligence. This is enough today. Let's continue tomorrow. You are full and I would prefer to let you digest this information, rather than pack in more."

After Henry withdrew from my consciousness, I mused on what he had said, some of which I knew, and some information I had never considered. Perhaps remembering the conscious state involved asking the right questions and contemplating the answers, so that the knowledge could permeate not only my mental but also my emotional and physical bodies. The moment I had this thought, I was flooded by a warm feeling of rightness and sensed the boundaries between my various bodies dissolving. This experience led to another cascade of knowing that this is how I could consciously assist in the process of transformation. And more to the point, knowing that my body intelligence was instrumental in encouraging this line of inquiry and was participating in the process.

I recalled Henry's words that the timing was right for allowing the boundaries to crumble between my unconscious and conscious states. I felt grateful that my body consciousness was assisting me, and through me others, to become who we were meant to be. By now a headache lurked in the shadows and, since I seldom experience headaches, I knew I was pushing and stopped. All would be revealed in its own perfect timing.

3

GLIDE IN NEUTRAL-POSITIVE WHEN LIFE TAKES A DIVE

Change what you can change, accept what you can't and have the wisdom to know the difference.

Serenity Prayer

The next morning, I was full of more questions to ask. Turning on the computer, I was caught in my first dilemma. There were several important emails seeking attention, or was it more important to speak with Henry at the same time each day? Would I interfere with the effectiveness of his transmission, if I sidetracked myself with other priorities? This dilemma was a recurring one; to do my or other people's priorities, and the niggling anxiety that sometimes occurred when caught in this situation.

Somehow, I realized that conforming to a rigid schedule with Henry was not the way to go. It was preferable to experiment with changing not 'what' to do, but 'why' I did something. Following this new practice, I might make the same decision but for different reasons. Whereas the former decision was based on fear, or habit, the latter decision was objective and allowing what felt best long-term. I trusted that Henry would agree with my observation and be patient while, in this case, I answered the emails.

Three productive hours later, I turned my attention inward to consider the most important question with which to start. I was musing on the 'best' question when Henry interrupted.

"We'll get to your questions in good time, but I want to discuss ways to move from being unconscious to being conscious. Body elementals don't recognize a separation between the unconscious and conscious states in the same way humans do. Even as we keep your lungs, heart and organs functioning—while you are sleeping or awake—we are aware of all thoughts and feelings that you unconsciously, or consciously, generate. Whether they are unconscious or conscious, positive or negative, they have the same effect on us; we program these thoughts and emotions into your body."

Immediately I thought of countless times when my initial thought or feeling about a person or situation was anything but positive. Too often my first feeling was discomfort or frustration. Henry must have picked up this thought but, through courtesy or compassion, didn't comment; so I asked him.

"Often I have a negative thought and feeling for a few seconds. This might happen when faced with a difficult person or situation, or these feelings pop up by themselves, when I'm alone, with seemingly no external trigger. The good news is that the moment I become aware of these negative thoughts, I correct them and regard them as an opportunity to grow more love, compassion and forgiveness for myself and others. When situations like this happen, do you program the negative initial thought and feeling, or the positive later one?"

"Both," he replied. "However, as positive thoughts align with universal consciousness, if the amount of energy is equal in both emotions, I would reinforce the latter, positive emotion."

"The strength of the energy being equal, you say. For many years, I've cultivated a non-attached state, which I refer to as neutral-positive, so that I'm not controlled by my emotions and can observe them more objectively. Is this a good thing to do?"

"What do you mean by 'neutral-positive'?" Henry requested.

"Neutral means being non-attached to roles I perform, such as spiritual teacher, friend, lover, meditator, writer, and feeling that there is a right or wrong way to be these things. Staying in neutral helps me to overcome fears that others will not approve of me. In this way, I become non-attached to the results of my life and work. By being neutral, I don't mean being indifferent. The western esoteric, H.P. Blavatsky, in her classic *The Secret Doctrine* said we shouldn't be in love, hate or indifference, meaning not to cling to any state.

"The positive in neutral-positive means that in the background of my thoughts I'm optimistic that the universe will give me wonderful things. For instance, the Dalai Lama's long-term goal is that Tibet will revert to the control of the Tibetan people and that he and other exiled Tibetans will be able to return to Tibet one day. But does he sit around moping about that hope? Absolutely not. Instead, he travels around the world teaching people about Tibetan Buddhism in a non-attached way. He says that he is not trying to convert individuals to Buddhism but wants to help them become more loving and peaceful, no matter what their religion.

"As I progress in the direction of the neutral non-attached state, in which the Dalai Lama is, I hear the voice of the universe more clearly and can align with it. The positive part of neutral-positive is faith, hope and trust that all will be well and that I'll receive either what I asked for, or better. In this space, my trust is unshakeable and effortless and contains peace and compassion."

"Insightful," Henry replied. "When you move into this non-attached state, you become more an observer and less a participant of the illusionary material world. In this non-attached state, there is a greater chance for you to become conscious in the moment because you have created more psychic space."

"Your answer begs another question. I've always wondered if it is better to be neutral-positive or to be only positive. What do you recommend?"

"That's a tricky one," he answered. "It depends on the situation as there are several factors to examine. Let's consider an example of where neutral-positive is the best course of action. If you have a deeply ingrained negative response to a person's negative actions towards you, let's say your mother-in-law, your ultimate goal is to become loving and compassionate towards her. Still, this may not occur easily and may take a great deal of time and effort. Although loving-compassion is the final goal, if you're able to move into neutral-positive, meaning to remain without an expectation that the relationship will improve, but with a wisp of hope, this is desirable and, at that moment, more doable.

"If your mother-in-law feels that you don't like her, it triggers negative reactions in her that, in turn, reinforce your negative feelings. This creates a downward spiral in the relationship. By moving into neutral-positive, you withdraw your negative projections and this creates psychic space for her to change. Her feelings of anger that you have taken her son away from her and guilt that she feels this way, coupled with fear that, if she doesn't change, she will lose her son are lessened by your neutrality. Your mother-in-law's change then triggers a positive reaction in you and elicits an upward spiral towards healing the relationship."

"I've found that relationships improve, just as you say, because of moving into a neutral-positive state," I commented. "I'd like to share another use for the neutral-positive state that folks have found helpful. When I don't initially achieve my goals, I view the situation as an opportunity to course correct—with non-attachment—until I'm able to find the right way to achieve the goal. Even if I never achieve my primary goal, I always achieve a secondary goal. That is knowing I've done the best I could, given what the circumstances allowed me to do. Through this attitude I continually feel successful."

"That's a great way to use neutral-positive," Henry affirmed.

"Back to my original question. Is it preferable to be neutral-positive or positive?"

"Okay. I'll give an illustration of when being positive is preferable," he replied. "I've heard people say that 'they are mirrors for others' and this statement is more accurate than they know. You are a mirror for others, so what are you reflecting back to them? This is the question that everyone needs to ask themselves. Are you reflecting back others' inadequacies, failures, lacks, or are you reflecting back to them their greatness? Are you celebrating with others the path they have walked and congratulating them on how well they have done? Are you strengthening their self-esteem, their confidence in themselves, while at the same time gently helping them to take their next step? This is how others rise to be the best that they can be. This is one way in which it's much better to be positive with others."

I smiled at Henry's example. "As a child," I said to him, "my parents joked about me, saying, 'You could talk Tanis into anything; she's so trusting. She believes anything people tell her.' To me, it seemed obvious that, if you think the best of people, they become their best; if you think the worst, that is what they become. In fact, I'm often kinder in thoughts about others than I am about myself."

"Jackpot," Henry exclaimed. "Actually, your weakness is common to most people and reflects a lack of self-worth. You feel unworthy of love and all good things."

"Suggestions are welcome," I said, feeling a bit like an insect caught in a spider's web. "Even if your assessment is valid, what is the solution?"

"First, it's important to not waste energy in guilt, shame and regret because, in doing so, you cling to a past that you can't change. Your energy is then lost in the present moment. Also, do not live for the future. Every thought and action that you take in the present creates your future. Live fully in the present and deal with the circumstances that surround you as best you can."

"It's difficult to live entirely in the present. Often my thoughts go to the past or future. Why is that?"

"The problem is fundamentally a lack of trust," Henry said. "When you don't receive what you want, do you trust that it's for the best?"

"Is it possible to trust the universe but not to trust that you've done everything you could? If so, you would feel that you have to do something to earn people's love and respect or, deeper still, to prove to the Infinite that you are worthy of life. Hypothetically speaking of course."

"What do you think is the solution?" he asked with an inner smile, obviously knowing I was referring to myself.

"Practicing neutral-positive helps a great deal. For example, say I have a goal and it is behind a door. I knock on the door and, if it opens, I go through. If it doesn't open, there are many other doors to knock on. I can return to the first door later, as sometimes I've discovered that I have the right goal but the wrong timing. I try to maintain the same non-attachment to the goal no matter how many times I knock on a closed door. I trust that universal consciousness knows what is best. By doing so, I've noticed that my trust and faith that I will be given wonderful opportunities—some that I would never have dreamed of—have grown stronger."

"Your approach demonstrates that you're moving towards consciousness, which I mentioned earlier. Shall I tell you why?"

Henry didn't wait for a response before launching in. "When you are in neutral-positive, your soul, the higher self, is able to download information to help you solve a problem. This is why folks have 'aha' moments when walking, showering and not dwelling on a problem. The answer then comes easily in an inspiration."

"Speaking of 'ahas'," I interrupted Henry, "When I am in a hazy, half-asleep state, waking up in the morning, I often receive answers to problems."

"That's because you are still partially in the astral realm, that you inhabit in the dream state and between incarnations. Individuals often enter the astral realm when daydreaming, walking or exercising. Moreover, it's possible to enter this astral plane consciously in your waking state and this happens when you are in neutral-positive. That plane has a higher frequency than that of the physical world and, by entering it consciously, not passively as in sleep, you advance your spiritual development. It's possible to go to higher than astral realms between incarnations but this depends on your ability to remain neutral, non-attached and yet compassionate establishing a consistent neutral-positive frequency."

"Great news!" I interjected. "This means, by maintaining a non-attached state, I and others increase our frequency, thereby, assisting our spiritual transformation."

"Absolutely. All emotions have frequencies. Negative emotions, such as anger, fear, guilt, shame, envy, lust and greed, delay consciousness whereas positive emotions, such as love, compassion, generosity, appreciation and devotion, assist in the development of consciousness. It's important not to give energy to negative emotions. By doing this, they lessen. Everyone has free will and you must use your will to transmute these lower emotions into the gold of the higher ones. By remaining in a neutral, non-attached state when confronted by a difficult situation rather than becoming angry or afraid, blocked energies in your cells are released. These energies then can be used to rise to higher states of consciousness."

"That's great and I want to use my free will however it's sometimes difficult to discern what is the best use of free will. We're back to my initial question. Is it better in difficult situations to be neutral-positive or fully positive?" I asked, still confused.

"You're funny," Henry said, amused. "You want a black-and-white answer and THAT is not helping your spiritual transformation. You evolve when you embrace both/and. It's a question of learning discernment about which emotional state is appropriate in which situation."

"I practice discernment and have discovered there are stages in its development."

"Say more."

"Here's an example of learning discernment. A man walks down a street and falls in a hole. The second time the man walks down the same street, he forgets about the hole and falls in again. The third time the man walks down the street, he remembers the hole, but forgets where it is and falls in. The fourth time, when the man decides to walk down another street, he has finally learned discernment."

"Great story but how does this relate to discernment in your life?"

"Good grief," I was thinking, "Is Henry ever exacting!"

"I am you, don't forget. This means that You are exacting."

I wasn't going to get away with clever anecdotes and might as well try to answer his question. "My discernment applies to how I use my energy. Some people I meet feel like an energy drain and I notice that they focus mostly on the negative, either about themselves, others or the world. Other people talk about things in which I'm not interested, like cars or sports, and I'd rather not spend time talking with them. I do not dislike them. I feel more neutral towards these folks and might even like them as people. Nonetheless, the truth be told, I would rather spend time speaking with people who have similar interests to mine. This feels more positive energetically. That's how I practice discernment."

"This is a good use of discernment because you seek people and situations that increase your energy, which, in turn, increases your consciousness," Henry said, before closing. "Let's stop our discussion now. That is enough information for today."

After Henry withdrew, I was exhausted. He was taking me into areas that I found intriguing and stimulating, so why was I tired? Considering this, I realized that he was pulling my thoughts and feelings from my unconscious into my conscious awareness. I felt exposed. I suddenly remembered that when our physical bodies die, no one judges us—not the Creator, St. Peter, angels, nor the ascended masters. Instead, we critique ourselves by accurately witnessing in a neutral-positive way when we did well and when we did not, according to our purpose in our last life. Henry was seeing me in this same way. He was not judging, only prodding the layers of self-protection for me to remove them. I needed to trust that, by doing so, his intention was to assist me to become fully conscious.

4

DO FEARS JERK YOUR LEASH?

*Who sees all beings in his own Self, and his
own Self in all beings, loses all fear.*

Isa Upanishad

Still digesting Henry's information, I decided to contemplate his words instead of starting a new topic. Two days later, fortified by coffee, I was ready to continue.

Picking up my thoughts, Henry initiated the conversation by saying, "Perhaps we're squeezing too much into one sitting. Doing more is not the right approach, if you do not have time to digest what we are discussing. Our conversations aren't meant to be a mental exercise but a transformational practice."

"I love to learn new things mentally; however, I seem to lag behind in emotional transformation based on assimilating the new idea."

"I couldn't put it better myself," he replied. I, on the other hand, would have preferred that he had disputed my comment.

"You're no different from the majority of humans. There is a time lag between people accepting a new idea in theory and them putting it into practice in their daily life. Do you know why?"

"Here we go again," I thought to myself. He knew how to dangle a carrot in front of the curious mind until I took a bite. "Go ahead," I said, "You know I'm interested."

"The mental realm has a much higher frequency than the emotional realm, so you're able to accept an idea in theory much quicker than to change your feelings about it, and even quicker than you can modify your behaviour in the physical realm, which has an even lower frequency.

This is why you are tired after our conversations. I'm helping you move into mental, emotional and physical coherence. Doing so increases your ability to manifest your goals; therefore, more than ever, it's essential that those goals are positive."

"Sounds good and I'm mentally on-board. What can I do physically to get there? It feels as if I have one foot on the ship and one foot on the shore and the ship has just sailed."

"Don't resist. The more you stay in neutral-positive, the more you naturally move into coherence. Shall I tell you what the underlying problem is?"

Seeing a second carrot dangling made me smile. "Ready and eager," I answered cheerfully.

"Fear is the greatest stumbling block for all humanity. It's the reason, in fact, that humans remain unconscious and in painful situations. Fear is the way the ego, the pain body, keeps you under its control. If humans only realized how great they are, they would be amazed. The ego fears that you will discover this, so it continually undermines you. Its favourite game is to inflate you and then shoot you down. It gets a bigger energy boost when it does this, because you climb higher and fall further. The ego lives off your emotional energy so it loves to create opportunities for you to feel anger, lust, greed, gluttony, sloth, pride and other negative emotions. Your solution is to remain in a neutral-positive, non-attached state—no matter what the triggers—and, by doing so, you deprive the ego of energy and it begins to shrink."

"I've studied and written about ways to overcome fear and have witnessed it shrink in myself. However, my body still feels fear when confronted by a new situation and, more often, by an old one where I've previously failed. Can you help me eliminate these last vestiges?" I inquired.

"That is exactly what we are doing. To a great extent, fear has been eliminated in your mental body through eliminating the thoughts that cause the fear. And you have mostly cleared the emotional body through the neutral-positive process and by developing compassion for others. The problem is that the fear is embedded in the physical body, in the cellular memory."

"Is this the same order for everyone or only me?" I inquired.

"You're not unique," Henry replied, a little too quickly. "The cellular memory of the physical body is the last area where fear is stuck for most people. That's why it's essential for you and others to work with their body intelligence to release it."

"Why is that?" I asked.

"Fears are part of the collective unconscious of humanity and body elementals program them into the genome of all humans when they incarnate."

"What do you mean by the 'collective unconscious of humanity'?" I asked, wanting to make sure I understood.

"Humans have been on the Earth for a very long time during which period they, led by fear and desires, have experienced a host of unpleasant thoughts from which even more unpleasant actions have resulted. Fortunately, they've also felt love, compassion and forgiveness. Every positive and negative thought and feeling leaves an energy signature imprinted on the ethers. Over time these energies, fuelled by new people adding their thoughts, gain strength and become thoughtforms that exist in the etheric memory of everyone's mental, emotional and physical bodies. People are unaware that these thoughtforms stimulate what they regard as their thoughts and feelings. This is what I refer to as the collective unconscious of humanity."

"Did I create these fear thoughtforms in previous lives that I now have to remove?" I asked concerned.

"You did create some of them, even if you are not conscious of this," Henry replied. "If your previous actions created fear in others, even if you were relatively fearless yourself, you are still responsible. This is how karma, the universal justice system, works."

"Have I repaid this karma and corrected the erroneous patterns in my present life?" I asked hopefully.

"Yes, many of them are erased and that is why you are mostly clear mentally of fear; however, once you do this individually, you have the additional responsibility to help your family, ancestors and collective unconscious of humanity to erase these fear thoughtforms."

"That doesn't seem fair. Why don't they clear their own thoughtforms?"

"You're right that each person needs to clear their own thoughtforms but sometimes they need help to understand WHY it is essential and HOW to do it. Humanity is going through a dark night of the soul presently. The collective karma of humanity is becoming increasingly obvious to most people because of what humans have done to the environment and to each other. Greater and greater numbers of individuals want to change but they don't know how, or are immobilized by fear. There are many ways to help free others from their negative thoughtforms such as praying for them, teaching them. Even writing a book, as we're doing, is a way to help."

"On a higher level I know that," I said, "but the little me is feeling overwhelmed. The idea of going through endless lifetimes clearing thoughtforms, not only my own but for others, often feels too much. Let's face it, it's incredibly difficult to give up one's familiar reality and what is known to leap empty-handed into the void of the unknown."

"The good news is that you and others are receiving bountiful energy from universal intelligence to assist in your spiritual transformation at this time. People are waking up as never before in the history of the world. And the more people that do so, the more energy is given to the collective unconscious to clear these old thoughtforms. You and others have free will to cooperate or resist the flow of destiny. Although the outside sometimes looks bleak, inside the cocoon of humanity great changes are occurring that are turning you into self-realized beings aligned with universal consciousness."

"Thanks for explaining and in my heart I feel what you say is true. We are waking up," I agreed. "Still, sometimes I feel that I've been working on clearing fear thoughts forever. They still aren't gone and I can't think of what else to do that will work."

"The ego loves to undermine self-worth to make people feel that they are never good enough or have not done enough," Henry answered. "Until you clear fear from your cells, the ego can use the patterns to regrow the emotional and mental fears, just as a weed regrows if you don't dig up the root. Clearing the physical body is the next step in your transformation."

"I have no idea how I would do that, if what I've done until now hasn't worked," I replied doubtfully.

"Part of the problem is your inherited family script, 'Try hard, don't succeed.' This script guarantees failure and is the ego's way of keeping you under its control. The solution is to stop efforting. Face every situation and role where you are attached to a specific outcome and let it go. Deep trust and surrender to universal consciousness remove all fear from the cells and eliminate ego control."

"It sounds like a deepening of the neutral-positive practice," I responded.

"It is—with one thing added," Henry replied. "You've learned through the practice to trust yourself, to trust others, and, to a great extent, to trust universal consciousness. This is all to the good. However, you still withhold a small part of what you think of as your identity from complete surrender. The ego fears annihilation with good reason, because it will be dissolved through this process. Surrendering to the will of the universe is the ultimate human fear, similar to the fear of dying, but remember that the ego is an illusion and there has never been separation from the whole."

"Could you give some examples of where to start?"

"Remember it's the ego—which is an overriding thoughtform that you and humanity have created—who is anxious. The ego is not the real you, the eternal 'I'. We will discuss the illusion of the ego in greater detail at another time, but now, I want you to focus on how you have created your fears. All fears are interrelated. If you dissolve one, the others begin to dissolve, but each fear exhibits a different frequency. Let's discuss the main human fears and how to dissolve them.

"The first one is the fear of the unknown as it stems from early human evolution when humans separated from infinite light and love and no longer felt safe. The environment was physically threatening and, if they didn't find food and shelter, they died. Fear of the unknown continues in the modern world and is reinforced by people's lack of love and connection with the Earth. The Earth lives in harmony with universal intelligence and, to be physically, emotionally and mentally healthy, humans must also do this.

"Natural law is the same as spiritual law and the Earth is a living being on the verge of becoming a conscious planet. The Earth's transformation catalyzes the transformation of all its beings, which are like cells in the body of the Earth. Nothing happens to the Earth that doesn't happen to humans and nothing happens to humans that doesn't happen to the Earth."

"I feel deeply connected to the Earth and don't understand how this relates to overcoming fears of the unknown," I said.

"Right, then. The solution to overcoming the fear of the unknown is to re-establish connection to Mother Earth in daily life. I call her 'Mother Earth' and it helps for you and others to actually think of the Earth as your mother who has given you life. To connect with her physically, I suggest walking in nature, gardening and anchoring your bare feet on the Earth. Emotionally, when you feel gratitude for your life on this beautiful planet, your connection to her is strengthened, as it is when you love and serve all her children, including humans, animals, trees, plants and the mineral kingdom. Humans won't harm the Earth if they feel this deep heart connection to her. In this way, you become the guardian of the Earth that you're intended to be."

"Is the fear of the unknown related to a fear of change that many individuals have?" I pondered.

"It is, but the fear of change has a slightly higher frequency. Fear of change is created by habit and is related to inertia and rote learning. Doing the same thing repeatedly gives a level of comfort, which is not bad in itself; nevertheless, it often leads to becoming unconscious. You increase your consciousness by embracing something new. Going on trips, meeting new people (especially those who are different from you), cooking different foods, and reading books outside of what you know, are a few things to sample. Doing this leads gradually to welcoming new experiences, which dissolves the fear of change."

"You're mentioning positive changes; however, many changes are imposed, such as being fired from your job, losing a loved one, or having a serious illness. Phenomena such as these create greater stress and fear," I interjected.

"They do; it's true," Henry replied. "Sometimes people are stuck and don't listen to the nudges from the universe about what they need to change, and thus they attract greater challenges to catapult them out of lethargy. This can happen when they stay in boring jobs because of fear of changing, or eat unhealthy foods, or think negative thoughts that cause illness. These difficulties have a silver lining, as the difficulties push people to return to harmony with the universe."

"Therefore, doing what we fear most is a way to avoid having painful situations imposed on us?" I suggested.

"In many cases that works but there is no escape from difficult situations, if it's your destiny to heal an erroneous pattern that might even be unconscious," he said. "This is where I come in as I can bring these patterns to conscious awareness through difficult situations, such as accidents, illness, divorce. In fact, to the entire gamut that you refer to as aspects of the dark night of the soul. In this way, difficulties help individuals to remove the blocks in their energy."

"Are you saying that you make people ill?"

"Not at all. People make themselves ill when their thoughts, feelings and behaviors are not in harmony with universal intelligence. I can only work with what people give me. Yet, not all illness is created from negative patterns. For example, a child may have a soul agreement to develop cancer to help his parents learn deeper love and compassion."

"That's a painful thing for parents to hear. Are you saying that a child may be more spiritually developed than his parents?"

"That's exactly what I'm saying. Pain is a part of your current reality and many advanced souls still have physical, psychological or spiritual pain. Don't judge another by the difficulties they face. Pain is sometimes employed by universal intelligence to catapult individuals more quickly into consciousness."

"That attitude is bound to attract folks in droves," I couldn't resist saying.

"Very funny. You and others receive exactly the right situation, as you well know, to succeed."

"Folks sometimes think that if they become spiritual they will escape difficulties," I said, trying to give Henry an insight into what it's like to be human. "It's puzzling for them when they discover that, although this is true in the long run, in the short run their difficulties may actually increase."

"In Japan the best swords are put in the fire and folded many times, not only once. It is the same for you and others. Each difficulty you overcome makes you stronger. You need this inner strength to hold increased spiritual energy which is the path out of pain."

"Thanks for explaining why we sometimes have difficulties without any obvious explanation. But I want to continue our discussion on fear because we haven't done my favourite—the fear of rejection," I said, welcoming any assistance.

"Some individuals, especially women," Henry commented, giving me a psychic nudge, "are attached to thinking that they have to be nice, gentle, kind and helpful to everyone and in every situation. This is most inappropriate when, for example, they really want to tell a non-stop talker to listen or they want to disagree with a racist's opinions. Their learned response is often programmed by religious, cultural and family scripts that leave them fearing rejection and abandonment if they say what they really feel.

"This fear, like many fears, originates in early human history when being abandoned could mean exclusion from the community and death. Such fears are almost always unrealistic in the western world but, by their very nature, fears make you think of the worst case scenario. The best, quickest approach you can take, if you have these scripts, is to be authentic, which means to do what you fear most. This doesn't mean to intentionally wound the person that you have a negative feeling about, but to honor yourself.

"For example, in the case I've mentioned, you could say to the individual who is causing you discomfort, 'I don't feel comfortable with what you're saying or doing.' You might even decide to give suggestions for improvement. Furthermore, if you either feel overwhelmed or that the individual has no intention of changing, you might want to save your energy and leave. You must examine your own unique situation to determine the cause of the difficulty, the solution and its gift."

"Is the fear of rejection in a higher frequency than the fear of change, which we discussed earlier?" I inquired.

"Fear of rejection," replied Henry, "is located in a higher frequency of the emotional body and is related to not loving yourself. When you love yourself unconditionally, you are authentic, secure and have intrinsic self-worth,"

"Easy to say, hard to do," I interjected.

"Because it's your big fear. But you have made progress in this area. When you were young, you avoided rejection by speaking only about topics where others felt comfortable. In doing so, you hid any differences you had to avoid rejection. You inherited your fear of rejection from your family, mostly your mother, who was conditioned by the era in which she was raised as well as her ancestral patterns. But you've confronted and destroyed a great deal of this fear since then."

"It wasn't always easy," I said, recalling those earlier days. "In my early thirties, my corporate clients fired me when they discovered I was leading past life regression workshops as, for them, I had lost credibility."

"Yes, but you confronted your fears of rejection and failure by deciding to continue giving these workshops, even when you lost most of your income and were rejected by people you cared for. To overcome any fears, it's fastest to do what you fear most."

"I was able to stand up for what I believed then because I felt, if I started compromising my spiritual beliefs, I would never stop. Also, my father was an outspoken man who never compromised his beliefs and thinking of him encouraged me."

"Every time you erase your fears," Henry remarked, "you clear your etheric body of negative patterns that I no longer need to program in you."

"When younger, I wanted to be loved by giving people something that they appreciated. I felt that my greatest gifts were spiritual and mental, not emotional or physical. Therefore, I gave others insights about how they could achieve their goals, thereby increasing their self-confidence."

"You gave from your strong area," countered Henry. "This is the way most individuals begin to confront their fears. It's a good starting place, but some never get beyond that approach. Your current strategy is more direct and more effective."

"Are you referring to my decision to express my real feelings and thoughts when I think it will benefit someone, even if the truth is uncomfortable for that person to hear and for me to say?"

"Yes. This behavior benefits both that person and yourself and it takes both of you into unknown territory in your relationship, so both of you must confront fears. Risking rejection is the fastest way to overcome your fear of rejection."

"I've received an amazing benefit by doing this, which I never anticipated," I said. "I feel more compassion and love towards others when I don't think that I 'must' be loving. Strangely, I also feel more love towards myself too."

"Your energy has increased dramatically through confronting your biggest fear. When folks are fearful, their energy is stuck, like a dam in the river that doesn't allow their energy to flow. Continue what you are doing, but I want to say more about the fear of failure.

"When someone—let's say 'he' for ease—has a fear of failure, he wants to be viewed as impressive in some way and is not as concerned that people like him. He might even use anger to intimidate and control others to get his way. At an earlier time in human history, this individual in a past life might have controlled others through fear, but in the modern world it no longer works. Now, if he uses anger to get his way, his wife might leave him, or he might be fired from his job. When this individual learns to control his anger, he starts to attract a positive, not negative, outcome. As he evolves, his fear dissolves."

"When you speak of a man getting angry, I distance myself from what you say, as if, being a woman, it does not apply to me," I commented. "Did you do that intentionally?"

"I wanted you to observe that one of your coping strategies, when your opinion and that of others differs, is to find the error in the other person's beliefs or actions rather than in yourself. Often, this is a favourite coping strategy for individuals who are in teaching and helping professions. They prefer to fix others, to see if it's safe and works, before applying the lessons in their own lives."

"Ugh," I replied. "Guilty as charged, although I wasn't fully conscious of your last point about making it safe for myself. From your words, I recognize that when I do this I turn the spotlight away from my life and issues and onto the other person. I've always believed that my motivation was to help that person. Now I see that the ego also wants to be in control. I may be keeping my world safe this way but, by keeping it small and closed, I keep the magic out."

"Absolutely!" Henry replied. "Any other insights?"

"We've discussed fears of the unknown, change, rejection and failure," I interjected before he could change to another topic. "Could there also be fear of success?"

"The fear of success is connected to fear of both rejection and failure. If you have fear of success, you likely underperform and don't break through the unseen barriers that you give yourself. This way you never fail to achieve your low aspirations. You might even feel guilty that you have more than others and don't want to draw this to other's attention for fear of rejection. Guilt prevents you from moving to the state of true abundance."

"What if you have enough money to do what you want?" I asked. "Why would you need more?"

"True abundance is not simply about money," Henry answered. "It's a frequency that allows the universe to give you everything it wants you to have, such as love, success and money, so that you can better fulfill your destiny. Limiting yourself is a version of scarcity mentality whereby you believe that by limiting the good things you receive, others will receive more. Others don't receive more because you limit yourself. In fact, the opposite is true. The more you limit yourself, the more you limit others.

"The secret to true abundance is for individuals to examine all ways in which they feel they don't have enough of something. This could be scarcity thinking about money, time, love, fun, sex, food … and these are only a few examples. Scarcity mentality strengthens thoughtforms of jealousy and greed, closes the heart, and creates separation between the haves and have nots. Once the scarcity is identified, the solution is to give where you feel scarcity."

"I've discovered," I commented, "that if I act as if there is abundance, fear decreases even if I don't necessarily receive more of the thing that I felt I lacked. The mindset changes so the fear dissolves. Are there any other fears you wish to consider?"

"Only one. The ego fears annihilation if it loses control. The ego is correct in this: it will disappear when you completely surrender your individual identity. At that time, all fears disappear and you are free.

"We've returned to where we started this discussion and the solution is to do what you fear the most. In this case, it means to surrender your attachment to being an individual. The feeling of me, my, mine is the root cause of scarcity. The fear of not having enough of something is how the ego creates desires that result in pain.

"I want to leave you with one key thought. Fears create energy blocks in your cellular and etheric bodies so that I cannot keep you healthy. As you eliminate these fears, your frequency increases and I am freed from constriction and can keep you healthy physically, emotionally, mentally and spiritually. That's enough for today, let's continue tomorrow. We're in new territory and I want you fresh."

By the time Henry left, I was exhausted. I felt like I was running a spiritual marathon and Henry was my coach. He wanted the best for me and was giving me tips on how to overcome my fears and wrest control from the ego but what hard work! I saw the importance of celebrating the progress I'd made in overcoming my fears of the unknown, change, rejection, failure, and success and knew that the fear of losing control was the one holding me currently.

I had identified with the ego's fear of losing control and made it my fear. In the blink of an eye I knew that my authentic self, my soul, the part of me that was deathless did not have this fear. It was obviously my ego's fear. The ego wanted me to keep this fear so it could control me. The way through this fear was, as I had learned so many times in the past, to do what I feared the most. What a freeing thought! What an invitation to creative, open, unboundaried adventure! To try new things that I'd never tried before. If I did this, any path would be a path of learning.

I remembered Jesus' words in Matthew 6:25-26 in the Bible, "Don't worry about everyday life—whether you have enough food and drink, or enough clothes to wear. Isn't life more than food, and the body more than clothing? Look at the birds. They don't plant or harvest or store food in barns, for your heavenly Father feeds them. And aren't you more valuable to him that they are?"

Jesus' words reminded me that I was loved just as I was. There was no reason to fear anything. There was no need to prove my worth to others, the Infinite, and certainly not to the false self, the ego. Obviously, it was time for a Guinness.

5

FREE YOURSELF FROM INHERITED LIFE SCRIPTS

We delight in the beauty of the butterfly, but rarely admit the changes it has gone through to achieve that beauty.

MAYA ANGELOU

I did a great deal of musing about our last conversation and the pain that fears cause and how that retards our evolution. It seemed like a Catch-22 with our fears strengthening the ego and the ego then strengthening our fears. Doing what we fear most and cultivating a neutral-positive approach to all situations helps, as does knowing that the ego is a fear-creating construct that needs to be dissolved, but I still felt deep-seated fear lurking in my physical body at a cellular level.

The next morning I checked out my self-assessment with Henry and asked about what to do.

"I'm always here," he replied to my inner question, "and there is nothing as important as what we are doing. The more insights you have, the more you loosen the hold of the ego. Then you can access even deeper insights. I've been waiting for this moment for many lifetimes. The entrenched fear you are thinking about is a thoughtform that regrows like a weed just when you think you've eliminated your fears. Thoughtforms are complex and composed of many thoughts and fears that make up your life script."

"Are my thoughtforms the same ones I've had for many lifetimes?" I asked curiously.

"Your thoughtforms are the same ones that ALL people have. The ego has a limited repertoire of fears and desires and, when you figure out what these are and what triggers them, you can eliminate them. Families develop favorite thoughtform patterns that become life scripts and these are handed down generation after generation through the DNA. These patterns go much further back in time than you might imagine. The mitochondria, known as the powerhouse of your cells, has DNA that originates in the chemical stew of Earth billions of years ago. Furthermore, I'm not merely referring to the physical genome. These patterns are created on the higher causal plane, where the soul resides. Then I program these patterns into the lower causal (mental) and astral (emotional) and physical bodies."

"What do you mean by 'causal plane'?" I interrupted wanting to make sure I understood his terms.

"A plane, or realm, consists of a certain range of frequencies. Every thought has a certain vibration that sets in motion a feeling that, in turn, creates a reaction in the physical body. This is how your thoughts create your reality. Your thoughts are on a lower causal plane. They exist in a range of frequencies higher than emotions, frequencies that in turn, are higher than physical frequencies. Is that clear now?"

"All clear," I responded, before asking, "Now could you give examples of some life scripts?"

"Many life scripts contain two messages," Henry replied. "One part may urge success and the second part, which may be either spoken or unspoken but implied, undermines success. A good example of a combination of a positive spoken and a negative implied life script is, 'Work hard but you won't succeed'. This script leads individuals into working hard but never reaching their goals. Their failure stems from low self-worth, the feeling that they don't deserve to be happy or get what they want. But, according to their script, they still have the desire to be happy and work hard to achieve it. Thus, like a rat in a maze, they go around and around, yearning and not receiving what they yearn for."

"I've read studies," I interrupted, "about how parents unconsciously say more negative than positive things to their children but, when confronted by the facts, they deny it. The parents state that they love their children and want them to be successful at attaining their goals but the parents unconsciously sabotage this from happening. For instance, if a child shows his or her report card with four As and one D, the parents might say, 'What happened here?' thereby emphasizing their disapproval. Or they compliment a child on something he or she does and then add, 'BUT... this one part isn't very good ... you can't earn a good living doing that ... no one will want it or ... someone else does it better.'"

"All men and women are affected by their family's scripts," added Henry. "Let's examine some common scripts and how they affect you. One is, 'A bird in the hand is worth two in the bush.' This script discourages individuals from taking risks with people and in life. This can make them overly cautious and reinforces their fear of change and fear of the unknown. A second one is, 'A penny saved is a penny earned,' which can reinforce stinginess and hoarding, because you feel there is never enough. Another self-limiting script is, 'Smile and the world smiles with you, cry and you cry alone.' With this life script, individuals might say only positive things to others and not share their difficulties with them. This script strengthens the fear of rejection."

"Umm. Seems to me that we can have many life scripts all competing for attention."

"A wonderful way of putting it," Henry said. "The ego uses conflicting messages in life scripts to keep you enthralled. If one script doesn't work in a situation, it can use another one to activate the pain body."

"But these scripts aren't entirely negative. For example, the script, 'Smile and the world smiles with you, cry and you cry alone' means that a person will be discouraged from being negative and will attempt to be optimistic and cheery."

"You're right of course," said Henry. "There are positive as well as negative aspects to life scripts. The important thing is to be authentic and true to your inner nature and not perform a role out of fear or pre-programming by your culture, religion or family. Everyone needs to do this in their life in order to de-program themselves from external influences. Let's talk about you. Have you chosen any goals for yourself that are part of your family's life scripts?"

"I bought my first home by the time I was 25, which would have been inconceivable for my parents—even though to own a home was one of their main goals. I can see now that I've fulfilled my parents' dreams at a much younger age. In addition, I'm self-employed. This is a family pattern on both my mother's and father's sides. I've achieved my family's life goals but, honestly, I wanted these goals myself too and don't feel these specific goals have diverted me from my path."

"It's very common for children to follow a family script to achieve family goals, while thinking they are their own goals. The children inherit the collective family thoughtform that wants someone to achieve the goals for the entire family. Thoughtforms have a kind of half-life so they are capable of energizing a limited range of thoughts and feelings in a person. Sometimes, as in your case, these life scripts increase self-esteem—which can be a good thing if the achieved goal is helpful on your life path—and sometimes they decrease self-esteem. Do you see any negative family patterns that operate in you?"

"I can see a major one. Until recently, I felt that I was lucky to have my parents as they did not have angry outbursts, drink to excess, or physically abuse or abandon us. I've been grateful to them as I know of the terrible abuses many children face. I always thought of them as 'good parents', but I've recognized lately an emotional absence that runs through my family. I think that both my parents were not emotionally supported or nourished at important times in their own lives, which led to closing their hearts at certain times. I'm not ascribing blame to them for they also were victims of their inherited family scripts. Not being loved unconditionally creates a lack of self-love and fear of abandonment. This appears to be the dominant life script operating on both my mother's and father's sides of the family."

"You are not alone. Most people's core wound is feeling unlovable and that they lack something that would make them lovable," Henry commented. "A core wound is a person's central issue and it is the foundation of the ego's power. From this wound, the ego creates desires, such as for money, success, recognition or sensory pleasures, to make the pain go away."

"And the solution is?" I inquired.

"Individuals, through inner contemplation, need to recognize the desire that is causing the pain, then release it. Focus on the cause instead of the symptom. For example, alcoholism or overeating is often caused by trying to numb or push down the pain of not feeling loved. By all means, individuals can go to groups that specialize in their addiction to receive helpful ideas and support but, ultimately, they need to lay bare the real issue. Recognizing how their issues stem from family scripts will help their body intelligence to release the stuck energy in their physical, emotional and mental bodies.

"This process is not a fun ride; it's a kind of purification and the ego fights to maintain control by continually triggering the core wound of feeling unloved. You have to move beyond self-blaming and blaming parents to deep forgiveness of yourself and them. You must continue to open your heart wider and wider to others and not be defensive, regardless of the outer or inner triggers."

"The more I consider my family scripts," I reflected, "the more I see that my parents' emotional absence was greater when I was a child, as few of their personal needs were met at that time. But, after they achieved their primary goal in buying their first house, they had more emotional energy to give to my brother and myself. During dinner, my brother and I were often asked our opinions and our parents listened and treated us with respect. This continued through adulthood."

"If individuals don't get many of their needs met," Henry said, "they keep their hearts closed. When they get their needs met and achieve some of their goals, their hearts open to give more love to others. It's important for parents and others to help children to achieve their goals because it leads to increased self-esteem. If people have self-esteem they are generous in helping others to achieve their goals and, in addition, self-esteem fosters a generous spirit that is contagious for others."

"I remember one of my parents' positive life scripts, which allowed me to overturn their negative scripts. It was: 'Think for yourself.' My parents reinforced my self-esteem by encouraging me to do this during our dinner talks. For example, my parents could not conceive of me going to university, as it was outside their realm of what was possible. They didn't object to me going but could not relate to it. However, when I did go and graduated, they were very proud of me."

"You were fortunate," he responded, "to receive a positive 'escape' script to throw out the negative self-limiting ones and your parents reinforced this script by their actions during dinner, which strengthened its message for you. If you don't receive a positive escape clause from your parents, you need to seek other sources, such as self-help books, practicing positive affirmations, finding a mentor, and avoiding situations and people that limit you.

"When you're stuck in a family script, you tend to see things in a two-dimensional, good or bad way. When you pull the script apart, it becomes three-dimensional and you can see the good and bad and everything in-between, as you uncover the truth without your wounded emotional filters. You are able to witness yourself and your family in an objective way with compassion. This is the path to healing, but there is something else I'd like to suggest as well."

"Your insights are helpful and I welcome other ideas," I replied with gratitude.

"When people first become interested in spiritual development, they may think that they need to downplay their physical and emotional needs for those of the spirit. However, they can only go so far spiritually before they must confront their own unconscious shadows. Eventually, everyone must look at their own darkness, anger, fear, hurts and lack of tolerance and transform these with their body intelligence's help. No one can do this for you. When you examine your own unresolved issues in the areas of pride, self-pity, worthlessness, jealousy and greed, your heart opens more fully in compassion for yourself and others. Working with deeper levels buried in your unconscious, you discover the seed from which these erroneous thoughts grew and, by then, you have released enough stuck energy that I'm able to erase these negative thoughtforms.

"Like an onion with many layers, you must work through even deeper layers of your unconscious in order to free yourself from attachments to others. Eventually you will no longer be manipulated by others, nor wish to manipulate them. In other words, you will live non-attachment. This is not the same as detachment, which is closing your heart to the other person. Instead, non-attachment is a deeply compassionate and understanding objectivity. If you don't learn this, the same pattern repeats itself either with the same or a new person."

"I've been working on this, but it sounds as if I have more to do," I replied.

"You've made progress, but I'm reminding you of what continues to be needed. These instructions are not only for you but also for others."

"I've noticed," I said, "that individuals often place themselves—unconsciously—in a position where they have an undesirable situation, such as a debt or quitting a job, in order to learn a lesson. They may also have attracted a person who is a teaching tyrant to teach them a lesson. This could be an alcoholic tyrant, a whiny tyrant, a dependent tyrant, or an angry tyrant. I've had my share of teaching tyrants and I guess I've been a teaching tyrant to others too. I've learned that, if I attract someone who is not to my liking, it says something about me and that I need to change my own pattern. I can't control whether the other person changes—that is the other person's choice."

"Relationships," he answered, "are wonderful ways to help individuals move to deep levels of their unconscious in order to bring negative thoughtforms to the surface so that they become conscious. There are two sides to any relationship breakdown and it's likely that both individuals are acting out scripted patterns from their parents, who, in turn, might be acting out the same scripts from their ancestors.

"Removing negative projections from others and accepting them in yourself is painful and takes courage. But it's the only journey worth taking, as it's the path to consciousness. When people fall in love, they often project overly positive thoughts and feelings onto their love interest and are unable to accept the 'real' person that emerges after a few months. Instead, they go from one relationship to the next, searching outside themselves for someone to make them happy. Scripts, which result in negative and positive thoughts and emotions, are not unique to individuals or even to their family. They stem from the collective unconscious of humanity and are handed down through genetic links as well as through cultural indoctrination by teachers, friends, religions. Therefore, when you and others deprogram yourselves, you help to deprogram all of humanity."

"My goal is unconditional love," I said, "but what that looks and feels like continues to change."

"Unconditional love is the optimal goal," Henry replied, "and it grows naturally as one evolves in consciousness. When you live in unconditional love, you have no fear or feeling of separation. When in union with universal love, you know the appropriateness of whatever you say, even if your words sometimes appear unkind. You're beyond being negative or positive, as it's viewed in the conditioned state in which most people live. As you become Love, you become neutral-positive and non-attached to how others perceive you, and your only motivation is to help free others from suffering.

"As individuals transform their own 'stuff' and learn non-attachment," he continued, "they become more intuitive because they no longer need armour to protect themselves from others. It takes a lot of energy to maintain incorrect thoughts and to hold back anger, repress hurt, and not talk about things that are bothering you, because you want to be seen as good and nice."

Pensively, I waited for him to say more.

"Although praying and meditating with this goal in mind helps, at the same time you need to be conscientious, consistent and persistent in cleaning up your own inner and outer garbage. Doing so results in a clearer sense of your soul's purpose. Once you are speaking and listening to your own note, you are able to tell when other people's notes are a little off pitch, when there is something that isn't quite correct in what they're saying or doing. You develop the gifts of clairvoyance, clairaudience and clairsentience to better see, hear and feel yourself and others. And the body intelligence is involved in every step a person takes to do this."

Henry's comments made me think of how important self-observation and witnessing my thoughts, emotions and actions had been in my life. "I've found that both myself and others go through stages in learning to self-witness," I said, explaining what I'd noticed.

"In stage one, we often unconsciously say or act in inappropriate ways. Stage two of developing a little more consciousness occurs when, in the process of speaking to someone, we think to ourselves, 'Oh no, I shouldn't be saying this!' At that time, we stop ourselves. In stage three, we ask ourselves before speaking, 'What would be the most beneficial thing for this person to hear right now?' Not what would make me look best or smartest, but what would be best for this other person. Then we say it. Stage four is when we no longer need to think of what to say and naturally say the most beneficial thing for the listener while staying non-attached to how the listener reacts to our words."

"Stage four, is the self-realized state," Henry commented. "It's common for individuals to move up and down in these stages and this becomes more obvious to you the closer you come to self-realization.

Have you noticed that you do this?"

"Unfortunately, I do," I replied. "However, I seldom feel guilty or punish myself when I don't behave in the best possible way and this, for me, is progress. Buddhist teachings speak about having right motivation for our actions, meaning that all our actions and thoughts are suffused with compassion, and that we have consciousness to *know* what our motivation is in every instant and *act* with right motivation. This is my ongoing goal. I believe that the universe gives us wonderful opportunities to practice right motivation and, even though circumstances may be painful and difficult, we're never given anything we cannot handle. Spirit wants us to succeed, not fail, so opportunities are given to us to develop consciousness."

"Witnessing yourself," he said, "is a very effective technique to separate from ego influence. The more that individuals can maintain this state, the less power the ego has. Ultimately, there will be no thoughts or comments from the ego, no mental chatter, only an inner stillness. All life themes and triggers are gone, nothing to do or not do."

"'Nothing to do or not do' sounds empty and undesirable to me. It reinforces my life script of abandonment and the emptiness I felt as a child. I've read enough stories by individuals who are self-realized—in union with the Absolute—about how wonderful it is. Therefore, on one hand, I know it will be great but, on the other hand, given my life script, it doesn't feel great."

"That is your major stumbling block—nurtured, once again, by your ego," he replied. "Your practices of self-witnessing, non-attachment, staying in neutral-positive, developing unconditional love, and having right motivation for your actions are powerful techniques to weaken the ego. You must persist and know that the closer you come to completely freeing yourself from the ego's illusion, the more difficult it is, as you have almost eliminated, or seriously reduced, most of the negative life scripts. In our next meeting, we will explore the negative beliefs that strengthen the thoughtforms which, in turn, create these self-limiting life scripts."

"What negative beliefs …?" I asked.

"Let's leave our discussion today on a positive note, shall we?"

Henry's comment reminded me of a valuable lesson that I needed to practice. That was: to stay in the present and trust that I had the right information and the correct amount to assimilate at any moment. With Henry's assistance, I was uncovering layers of insights that had been undiscovered until now. Oh yes, I had previously known bits and pieces, however the pattern of the whole was now revealing itself. I saw more clearly the life scripts I was living. By witnessing these in a neutral state, something buried and knotted was releasing itself in my psyche.

6

NEGATIVE BELIEFS ... BEGONE!

*Spiritual evolution occurs as the result of removing obstacles
and not actively acquiring anything new.*
DAVID HAWKINS, *The Eye of the I*

"Good morning," Henry began. "Before we dive deeper into underlying beliefs that inhibit spiritual progress, I want to give a cautionary message. Without exception, the best way to facilitate consciousness is not to fight the ego through resisting lower qualities, but to embrace positive higher qualities."

"That's a bit vague. Can you tell me what you mean by a 'quality'?" I inquired.

"A 'quality' is a belief, a point of view, and it can be about self, others or universal intelligence. Every belief creates a positive or negative feeling that, in turn, results in a certain frequency. Imagine a scale from one to 10. One is complete ego enthrallment in this illusionary world, in a state of pain and suffering, and 10 is being self-realized in union with universal consciousness, in a state of peace and bliss. On this scale, your beliefs about yourself might create a frequency of 8, your beliefs about others might be 5 and of universal consciousness an 8. This means that your overall level of consciousness is brought down by your beliefs about others. For example, you might trust yourself and the universe more than you trust others.

"Furthermore, conscious beliefs are only the tip of the iceberg. Individuals may have many more unconscious beliefs that create their frequencies. After people clear their conscious beliefs, they still need to clear their unconscious beliefs and the first step is to encourage these to surface, which is what we are doing together."

"The techniques of surrender, neutral-positive and non-attachment are designed to clear the unconscious, aren't they?" I inquired.

"Those and others," Henry replied. "One of these 'others' is yearning to unite with universal consciousness. This desire fuels your willpower to remove any obstacles that inhibit this, be these attachments to family, possessions or physical pleasures. In fact, one of the easiest times to unite with the Infinite is when, near death, you release all attachments. The difficulty in waiting until you're near death is that, unless you've cleared your unconscious beliefs and self-views, they will be carried into your next life."

"Does everyone's body intelligence encourage them to examine their unconscious beliefs?" I asked.

"Until individuals' frequencies are at a certain level, they are only interested in correcting their erroneous conscious patterns. But once they've done this and discover they are still unhappy, they begin to examine their unconscious beliefs. We, being spirit in bodily form, eagerly await this time and will help them."

"Beliefs start in the womb," I interjected, "when the baby picks up the thoughts and feelings of his or her mother. I remember doing this and I don't think I'm alone. Sensing my mother's fear, related to the difficulties in having an unplanned child, I sent her reassuring thoughts, of being such a good daughter, that she'd be happy she had me. This desire to do what makes your parents happy—in order to be safe—continues through childhood and even into adulthood. We accept beliefs and adopt qualities that we think our parents want from us."

"Even children," explained Henry, "who act out against parental beliefs, are still programmed by them. When they resist their parents' beliefs—because they are physically or mentally incapable of fulfilling them—they often think of themselves as 'bad'. For instance, if a parent wants you to be a doctor and it's not possible academically, you may feel bad about yourself, your parents, or both. This can lead either to not trusting yourself, if you feel your parent's beliefs and goals are good ones, or not trusting your parents, if you don't respect them or if their goals are contrary to yours. Another case in point is if your mother wants you to be a flight attendant, because she wanted to do this herself and never had the opportunity, and your father wants you to be an engineer, as he thinks it will guarantee job security.

If neither of these goals appeals to you, you find yourself in an untenable position of disappointing your parents. This may result in negative feelings from them or yourself."

"Also," I picked up from where he left off, "sometimes parents say one thing and do another. For example, parents may tell their children to be generous to others, yet are selfish themselves. This hypocritical behavior makes a greater impression on the child than the stated belief. Individuals may not be intentionally hypocritical, but they still have conflicting beliefs. "For example, two of my conflicting beliefs are 'The universe wants me to have everything I want' versus 'I can't have what I want.' Since becoming aware of these conflicting beliefs, I've sought to dissolve the self-limiting one by practicing abundance behaviors that aren't based on scarcity. This technique works, but it takes a long time."

"That's because of another one of your erroneous beliefs ... that it will take a long time," Henry commented. "People have multiple beliefs that lead to a life view or way of thinking that they use when considering anything that touches on that life view. Dismantling them, one at a time, is not as efficient as changing the entire paradigm, the self and life view, that houses that set of beliefs."

"It may be difficult to change a paradigm," I suggested. "This is especially true when we aren't aware that our view of ourselves and others encompasses our approach to our entire life. Even scientists realize that their conscious and unconscious thoughts and biases may affect the results of their experiments and that they might only see the results that they expect to get. For example, if the scientist, or anyone for that matter, has a paradigm that says if you can't see something, it isn't real, then everything that is unseen is therefore negated. The problem is that even when we change our paradigm, we might become fixed in the new one and stop progressing in consciousness."

"Truth evolves as beliefs evolve and you need to continually challenge your current paradigms so they don't become locked," he added. "When you change many small beliefs, your condition changes, and, at a certain point, you jump to a new paradigm, one with a higher frequency. This is how evolution works and it quickens as you move to even higher states. Also, the higher your frequency, the more you have a positive effect on the collective unconscious of your family and of humanity in general, which results in them also rising to higher paradigms."

"Is this why we are often surprised by how much our parents' beliefs change from the beliefs of the parents we knew as children?"

"Exactly! For instance, what if someone's parents are prejudiced against homosexuals and then their child turns out to be homosexual. The parents have a choice either to change their self and life-view or to lose their child. If individuals experience enough of these changes to their beliefs, they change their entire paradigm."

"Question?" Etherically I waved my hand in the air.

"Can people move down into a lower paradigm as well as up?"

"Unfortunately they can," he responded. "If people have enough setbacks and crises in their lives, they may choose to move to a lower paradigm. They always have free will."

"Do you program these possible paradigm jumps or setbacks into the DNA of the fetus before the ego is developed?" I asked.

"The programming starts during conception, when I program the life purpose into the fertilized egg. Both negative and positive ego qualities are given to the genome; they only wait for outer circumstances to cause them to bloom. Individuals in their higher Self, accompanied by karmic advisors, choose parents based on the necessary karmic DNA and epigenetic patterns that are necessary for the individuals to fulfill their destiny. Circumstances in their life, such as their environment and lifestyle, turn the DNA codes off or on in their body. Individuals are repeatedly born into group pods that are often referred to as soul groups. That way, they inherit similar life scripts to this group. The group might include parents, extended family, friends and also allies on a similar path. Gradually, as one's consciousness increases, it spreads in a network of light to include other soul groups and ultimately all humanity and beings on the Earth—not only in the physical but also in other realms."

"That's all good news but I'm wondering about something," I inserted. "Is our life predestined by the program you give us at conception or have we free will to change it?"

"All individuals have free will and are given the opportunity to change their patterns while incarnated. Also, because thoughts and feelings dwell in the causal and astral realms where time and space are non-existent, when individuals move to a higher consciousness, they change their ancestral pattern both backward and forward in time. This means they help erase the self-limiting scripts for their ancestors and descendants as well as for their group pod."

"I'm happy to hear this. Until now," I asserted, "I've focused on clearing my astral and causal bodies. At this point, I'm interested in clearing these core beliefs in the cells of my physical body. If I do this, will it also help my ancestors?"

"You're in luck! That is the specialty of all body intelligences. Let me explain how it works. Each thought you have creates either a comfortable or uncomfortable feeling in your body. Even unconscious thoughts create a physical feeling. To determine what thoughts you have, pay attention to how your body feels. I can't stress this point too strongly! Then, trace the positive or negative feeling back to what was happening—either in your outer environment to trigger the feeling or internally to what you were thinking—if you cannot discover an external trigger."

"What if a feeling is pleasurable," I remarked, "but you don't want to lower your frequency? For example, thinking about sex is pleasurable, yet you don't want to dwell on it, especially in business meetings."

"Understood!" Henry said, with what felt like a smile. "But acknowledging the feeling does not mean you have to energize it. Feeling frustrated or disappointed with yourself for having undesirable feelings only gives the ego more power, more energy, and keeps your attention in the duality of good and bad, which is the ego's home ground. It's preferable to create a mental space between the feeling and your thought about the feeling. This space is where the witness, which is the soul, resides. In this space, you're able to observe the feeling and not energize it."

"Could you define what you mean by the 'witness'?"

"The witness is your soul, your higher self. The witness is objective and is able to see your patterns, beliefs and thoughts and the underlying reasons for them. Everyone needs to develop their witness on the journey to consciousness. It allows you to free yourself from unwanted beliefs and thoughts by staying in neutral and not energizing them.

"Now I want to discuss," he continued, "other ways to eliminate low vibrational beliefs and feelings as most have a positive quality at their root."

"Amazing," I interrupted. "I discovered this in my 30s when meditating on the seven deadly sins and found the positive gold nugget within each of them. When I discovered the positive quality, I embraced it in my heart and, in doing so, dissolved the negative aspect."

"An excellent technique. When you did this, I had an open door to transform your consciousness very quickly, because you freed the energy trapped in lower thoughtforms and allowed me to move your energy into a higher state."

"Which of these sins have the lowest frequency?" I inquired.

"Before answering your question, I want to point out that the word 'sin' comes from the Anglo-Saxon meaning 'to miss the mark'. It was a term used when arrows did not hit the target. The reason I bring this to your attention is to remind you that ALL frequencies are aspects of consciousness. However, higher ones are associated with enlightened states, whereas lower ones bind you to the illusionary world of pain and suffering and 'miss the mark'."

"Now to answer your question," Henry said, returning to my query. "Let's look at self-views and beliefs that are self-destructive and life denying. Two of the most destructive are shame and guilt. Thoughtforms of shame and guilt usually reside in the lower part of your body. They close the lower chakras which are the etheric portals I use to feed your lower physical organs. Because the access to reproductive and digestive systems is blocked, illness and disease sometimes result.

"Both shame and guilt create low self-esteem but how each is created may differ. Physical, sexual or emotional abuse can create shame, which leads the victim to feeling unworthy of happiness and, in its most severe form, unworthy of life itself. Guilt, on the other hand, can result from feeling that you are disappointing others, be it parents, your spouse or God—which is religious guilt. Guilt can create fundamentalism where you project your guilt onto others, thereby making others wrong."

I was busy absorbing what Henry had said and was doing a quick inner check on my lower organs, when he asked me, "How do you help someone overwhelmed by shame or guilt?"

"If individuals have shame or guilt that creates low self-esteem," I replied,

"I attempt to find something they've accomplished and then link another goal they want to the feeling of success they have from achieving the first goal. The key is to meet them where they are and encourage them to do something they believe they can do.

"I have a general question before we go on," I added. "When interacting with people whose self-views and beliefs differ from mine, I try to create a bridge to them by stressing similar beliefs, instead of emphasizing our differences. Is this a good idea?"

"Creating a bridge between you and another is a good way to diffuse the ego," he replied. "It's essential to remember that the soul of each person is pure. This is the place to meet everyone. The preferable attitude, in most situations, is one of unconditional love and acceptance of the person—even when you are suggesting a behavior change.

"Let's examine another destructive self-view, shall we? Sloth, what you call laziness, is characterized by hopelessness, despair and numbness. What would you recommend to help move someone out of laziness?"

"I'd rather give examples of negative qualities and you give solutions!" I joked.

A long pause ensued. He wasn't buying in, so I tackled his question. "I think that the core problem with laziness is feeling that you can't have what you want, so why try. This belief might even be systemic, created through ancestral poverty or racial discrimination. To get momentum going, I might recommend giving yourself something you want, even if it is superficial, like clothes or a massage. Once you know that you can have what you want, attempt larger—hopefully higher—vibrational goals."

"How would you help a person whose laziness is caused by hopelessness and despair?" he prodded me to go deeper.

"Feelings of hopelessness might be a transitory state that accompanies the dark night of the soul. If this is the case, I would help the person to understand that the dark night is actually a stage in the spiritual journey and re-contextualize it as a sign of progress to give the person hope that it will pass."

"But what if the person is stuck in grief and sadness as a dominant self-view?" Henry responded, sticking to his point. "Perhaps, the person has lost a loved one through death or abandonment. Comments?"

"If the hopelessness and despair are part of a self-view, I would try to light a fire under the person. This may seem hard-hearted, but sometimes I think stuck grief is an attachment to the belief that something is owed you, that someone has to make you happy, be it a spouse, parent, your children, or even the government. This is an illusionary fantasy, which only perpetuates pain, as you live in continual disappointment. This person feels alone and wants love but, ultimately, the only love that is guaranteed is from universal intelligence. Meditation and prayer would also help this person to maintain a neutral-positive attitude to outside circumstances and to accept 'what is', which will increase his or her vibration. That said, grief can be a natural feeling due to loss, as long as the person does not get stuck in it. Isn't that correct?"

"Grief is natural for the ego," he countered, "but not for the soul that exists, regardless of external circumstances, in the eternal presence of joy. We've previously discussed the negative feelings of fear and anxiety and their solutions, so let's talk now about three more negative approaches to life: greed, gluttony and lust. What would you say is the erroneous belief underlying these?"

"Both the Bhagavad Gita and the Vedic sage Patanjali," I offered, "refer to craving sense pleasures, such as these, as impediments. In this, they agree with Christian doctrine. With gluttony, you want more food, with lust more sex. Greed, too, is a kind of gluttony and greed could be in any area, because you want more for yourself and are never satisfied. You could be greedy for fame, money, material goods, status, power, love, the list goes on. Obviously, some of these things are necessary in order to live but not with any attachment. How am I doing?"

"The jury's out. I want to hear more before commenting," he joked, prodding me.

"We need money for food and shelter," I continued. "And if we have physical and financial resources, we might be able to do more good for the world. Craving these things is the real problem and it's easy for the ego to create this in us, given that our economy in the modern world is built on the belief that 'more is better'. My intuition is that separation from universal consciousness, with the emptiness this brings, is the root cause of craving. If so, the solution is to trust that there's enough to fulfill our life's purpose and to surrender everything to which we're attached."

"What is the desire from which craving stems?"

"Desire to reunite with the Source from which all happiness comes," I replied, hopefully.

"That's true, which brings us to the next negative quality: anger."

"Anger," I responded, "might stem from not having what you want, such as others agreeing with your point of view. The ego wants to be in control and may feel attacked if others do not agree with you, so it defends itself by getting angry. This causes an adrenaline rush that gives the ego more energy which it loves. Anger, whether expressed or not, can also be linked to feelings of envy, another one of the seven deadly sins. You might feel that someone has something that you don't, like material goods, beauty, friends, but it could also be that they have more fun, more time, etc. The erroneous belief is based on separation and a lack of trust in the universe to give you exactly what you need."

"And what about pride?"

"The Bhagavad Gita," I replied, laughing at my pride in being well-read, "refers to pride as self-conceit and insolence. I think the erroneous self-view is that of being better than others. Feeling that you are smarter, richer, kinder, purer and even spiritual pride of feeling you're closer to enlightenment than others all lead to feelings of comparison and separation from others. The positive gold nugget in pride—even when unconscious—could be a desire to prove that you are worthy of love, not only from others but ultimately from the universe."

"What are your conclusions from our discussion?"

"Your turn," I suggested. I wanted feedback to learn if my beliefs and thoughts were on the right track or not.

"The ego knows only separateness," Henry began, "which creates all negative beliefs and, from them, feelings. The ego can never give supreme happiness. Only the soul, and consciousness working through the soul, can do this. When you no longer search for happiness in the illusionary world, universal will, which is always in you and with you, becomes your guide."

"And how are you involved with this process?"

"I have two main functions," Henry replied. "On behalf of universal consciousness, I act as your conscience and guide to assist with your journey.

In this context, you think of me as body spirit. Also, as the body intelligence who builds and maintains your physical, emotional and mental bodies, I have a biological function."

"I'm curious to know how thoughts and feelings affect the health of the physical body," I inserted, with hope that Henry would answer that question.

"That's a large topic and best left until we speak about the brain and heart," he answered, concluding our discussion.

Henry's strategy of asking me to answer my own questions was a great teaching. What a good reminder that our answers lie inside us and that searching outside ourselves for answers and happiness is misguided. Unfortunately, even if our questions and answers lie within us, they don't come in matched sets. The ego keeps us thinking that there is some secret that, if we only find it, will lead to happiness. Increasingly, during our discussion, I was reminded that by detaching from the ego's drama created by negative beliefs, we shatter the illusion it creates. To do this, we only need to listen to the deep truth we already know in our higher self, our conscience, our small inner voice.

7

ARE YOUR LOVE, WISDOM
AND WILL EQUAL?

*Love is lying in wait in your own heart. You only
need to abide in truth. You need only be still.*

Prajnaparamita

The next day, I was looking forward to hearing the scientific explanation about how my body intelligence, the body elemental, works biologically to program me. This was not to be, as Henry immediately launched into a description of positive qualities that promote consciousness.

"The two topics are the same," Henry said, when he felt my disappointment. "Positive qualities release energy blocks in your cells. Because of this, I'm able to move you to higher frequencies. This is a biological function. Humans love to segment thoughts, feelings and biological functions into different categories, but all is ONE. Your view of the Infinite affects the frequency of your thoughts, emotions and physical body."

"I don't understand how someone's view of the Infinite affects their frequency." I said, puzzled.

"No problem. I'll explain," he replied. "Let's examine the difference between the way the Infinite is represented in the Old and New Testaments of the Bible and, for consistency, I'll use the Christian terms. In the Old Testament, God is seen as punitive and vengeful if he is not obeyed. The people of Sodom and Gomorrah are killed, the Temple of Babylon is torn down, the tablets of Moses are broken and poor old Job, who is a righteous man, is not righteous enough, so he is put through continual suffering. This God-view creates a life view in people of anxiety, fear and anger.

The God-view of the New Testament, conversely, is about love, compassion, forgiveness and peace—qualities that create in people very different life views and emotions. All religions show a similar progression. They evolve as their followers evolve."

"Your explanation tallies with astrology," I commented. "Every two thousand years is devoted to a different astrological sign and set of qualities that humanity needs to develop. The Old Testament reflects the qualities of the two thousand years prior to the birth of Christ. The New Testament reflects the next two thousand years up to the present. We're now entering the Aquarian Age. What qualities and God-view does humanity need to develop during this coming time?"

"The next two thousand years of the Aquarian Age," Henry answered, "will witness the awakening of humanity. You've always been One with the Infinite but have forgotten this in your dream of separation. Soon, you'll awaken from that dream. I haven't chosen the topics of our conversations randomly. They are exactly what is needed for you and others to embrace the qualities of the Aquarian age. Each individual has free will to choose to facilitate this process, resist this process, or attempt to ignore this process."

"So what's going to happen to people, such as agnostics and atheists, if they don't believe in a God? Not even the Old or New Testament versions, let alone the Aquarian one?" I inquired with concern.

"Atheists and agnostics are not the same," Henry answered. "Whereas atheists in the narrowest sense of the word actively negate the possibility of an all-intelligent Source from which all else is derived and of which we are One, agnostics neither believe nor disbelieve in a supreme Source as they claim humans cannot know if it does or does not exist. Both atheists and agnostics are similar in believing that they are in control of their life. Their life view relies on the ego and material world, which is the ultimate illusion. Agnostics and atheists may be kind to others because they have learned this from parents or society and, by doing so, their ego needs get met more easily. But their view of the Infinite does not lead directly to consciousness."

"Where does science stand with regard to the Infinite?" I inquired.

"There's a difference between science and being a scientist," Henry replied. "A person could be an atheist, agnostic or self-realized and still be a scientist."

"Okay, I follow what you're saying about our view of the Infinite either helping or impeding our path to consciousness. This information is great to know in theory but I'm more interested in what I and others can do to, as you say, 'facilitate the process'. I may believe we are entering the Aquarian Age where I and others will be self-realized but can I rest on my haunches and do nothing and still get there?"

"Good point," Henry acknowledged. "I'll be more specific. There are as many paths to self-realization as there are individuals but let's consider the three main paths: the path of love, wisdom or will, the latter one being active service in the world. These paths are often not distinct and an individual may choose a blended path of more than one of these. Although the path of love more obviously is the path of the uncaged heart, the other two paths—that of wisdom and that of using your will to serve others—also open your heart."

"I can relate to what you're saying now," I interjected, "because I've noticed that individuals incarnate with one of these paths stronger than the others. For some, the difference is slight but, for many, it is more noticeable. For instance, when a person's strongest path is love, he was likely a cuddler as a child, always hugging others and demonstrating affection. The most difficult discipline for this child to receive was disapproval and to be sent to his room, isolated from others."

"What about the child born with wisdom?" Henry asked.

"The child born with wisdom has a cooler personality, enjoys watching others and learns how to behave from this. This child is often wiser than his years and might even be described as a 'know-it-all' or 'smarty-pants' by parents who are often astounded by the wisdom of this child. This child enjoys time alone, reading and/or communing with nature."

"And what would you say about a child with strong will?"

"A child with will as his strongest path is a natural leader and other children gravitate to him. When playing games, the child with strong will decides the roles for playmates and who will be part of the group and who not. This self-confidence will stand him in good stead in life. Through the strength of his will, he will not be crushed by setbacks and will attain his goals more often than individuals on the other two paths. As a parent, the best way to appeal to this child is to be firm and fair. This child will manipulate or ignore a weak parent or other authority figures, but respect those who have earned his respect."

"Your perceptions are correct for children, but have you noticed changes later in life?" he asked.

"I have indeed. Regardless of our strongest path at birth, the early part of our life—generally to middle age—is devoted to developing our second path. Therefore, a child born with love might develop either wisdom or will next, and one born with will might choose to develop love next. This decision might be conscious or unconscious, as learning to be safe and succeed in the world helps to inform our choices.

"I've noticed that sometime in middle age," I continued, "after we've developed our second quality as well as a strong ego to succeed in the world, a crisis of meaning occurs. This might be called a mid-life crisis or a dark night of the soul. The personality has grown as much as it can and, like a baby chick, it cracks its shell so that it can better access soul consciousness. Often this crisis forces us to develop the third quality. We realize that we must develop our third, least preferred quality, when the other two no longer work in our lives to get us what we want. During this time, when we're thrown back on our weakest quality, our personality feels very insecure. It's unhappy because it no longer knows how to get what it wants. Only the soul has the answer to happiness and this answer lies outside the ego's control. We refer to this crisis as a dark night of the soul but it's really a dark night of the ego."

"You and others," Henry commented, "must develop all three qualities to become a conscious creator. If you've only developed love, you might be unconditionally loving but lack discernment. For example, you might attract individuals who want to be taken care of and who don't want to take responsibility for their lives. You aren't helping these people by approving of their unacceptable behavior. On the other hand, if you develop only wisdom, you might have the right answer, but others won't listen because they see you as cold and not having their best interest at heart. Lastly, if you develop will, without the moderating influence of the other two qualities, you're dangerous. You'll likely have an over-developed ego that greedily takes what it wants from others with no concern for them."

"It's easy to see," I said, "that individuals with over-developed will and a lack of empathy and compassion for others have led our world astray and that's why many good people are afraid of using their will. Yet, I think it's essential that we use our will to act and, by not doing so, our love and wisdom aren't as effective as they could be. We are not full creators. We need to develop all three paths: love, wisdom and will, not just for our life in this material world but to free ourselves from this illusionary world."

"Very true," Henry replied. "And to more deeply understand the importance of these three qualities, you need to look beyond the physical world to the etheric. The key to spiritual transformation lies in moving from the lower frequency of your physical heart, controlled by the ego's desires, to the higher frequency of your etheric heart. A three-fold flame of love, wisdom and will resides in your etheric heart. This flame expands as you become more conscious and, eventually, you become all flame. Since early times, this light has been depicted by artists as halos around the heads and bodies of saints. It's possible for self-realization to occur through mainly one of the three paths, that of love, wisdom or will; yet, it's preferable to balance all three qualities, especially if you wish to remain in the world to assist others."

I must have looked vague, as Henry continued.

"The importance of these three qualities is emphasized in many spiritual traditions. For example, the Bhagavad-Gita, the sacred text of the Hindus, speaks about these three paths to consciousness. These paths are referred to as Jnana, Bhakti and Karma (wisdom, love and right action through will). There is a fourth path, called Raja, or kingly yoga, that combines meditation in addition to these three paths. Raja is an excellent path to follow to uncage your heart as it is usually the fastest one."

"I've noticed," I began, "that each path has its dangers if we become attached to it—which is what the ego wants. For example, the path of Jnana (wisdom)—that of the intellect—entails the danger of not surrendering your thoughts (your mind), which is still the ego, to move to higher consciousness. The path of Bhakti (love) is devotion and deep faith in the Infinite, but the danger is becoming attached to feelings of bliss and not surrendering these to move beyond self-identity. The path of Karma is service to others, but the danger is helping others in order to feel good about yourself, which is ego, to the exclusion of doing what universal will requests. There is even another path, Hatha yoga, that you did not mention. Its foundation is physical postures, but the danger is attachment to having a perfect physical body. A larger danger, to my way of thinking, is that spiritual seekers may dabble in all these paths and never commit long enough to any of them to make substantial spiritual progress."

"You," Henry said, "have put your finger on the difference between the external and internal aspects in all these paths. Often people follow external forms of their chosen path first but, ultimately, they must turn their gaze inward. That is what we are doing in our discussions."

"But, as far as I can see, our discussions are bouncing among all the paths and are not sticking to one," I commented, confused.

"That's right," Henry affirmed. "Because the positive qualities that you and others need to develop are usually associated with one or another of these paths. However, all the paths are ultimately interconnected."

"Good Heavens. First you speak about views of the Infinite, then the main paths to consciousness, and only now we get to actual qualities that one needs to become conscious. Could we please speak about positive qualities that lead to consciousness, regardless of the path to which individuals are drawn?"

"Happy to oblige," Henry said, sending me loving energy. "Practicing positive qualities, no matter which spiritual path or tradition you follow, will increase your frequency. Let me explain with the quality of willpower. Will might also be referred to as steadfastness, perseverance and commitment. They are all basically the same quality. Will alone is seldom enough to free yourself from the ego and it needs to be balanced by the quality of devotion. Will is more yang and devotion more yin. If you are too yin, you may never accomplish anything and, if you are too yang, you empower the ego.

"However, will and devotion, by themselves, may not lead to union with the Infinite. First, you need faith and trust that the Infinite is unconditionally loving and preferable to the ego state you currently inhabit, or you will not wish to surrender your ego to unite with it. The positive qualities of faith and trust create a foundation for devotion. Likewise, faith and trust—that it is possible for you to re-unite with the Infinite—are the foundation for will."

"Thanks for explaining how faith, trust, devotion and will reinforce and support each other. Could you mention the interconnection between other positive qualities that lead to consciousness?" I asked.

"As you analyze your life," Henry replied, "you discover that you are far from perfect, so you learn humility. Through humility, you learn to understand and forgive yourself and others for the pain you and they have caused. Through this process, you become compassionate and wise. Through wisdom, you seek to lead your life through alignment to consciousness, which leads ultimately to peace."

"From your examples," I remarked, "I now understand that it does not matter which positive quality you develop first, because they are intertwined like strands of a rope. Each quality is needed to make the rope stronger."

"That's a good metaphor. The rope works best when all strands are of equal size and it helps to develop all these qualities, not just the ones that are easiest for you because of your temperament. These qualities all facilitate awakening from your dream of individuality and separateness. The universe will reflect back to you the qualities that are weak and need to be strengthened, as well as the ones that are too strong and need to be softened. For example, if you have learned universal law intellectually and believe yourself to be wise, but you have not learned humility, opportunities will occur to learn it. So, you might have a stroke or develop Alzheimer's so your mind is compromised."

"That's kind of drastic, isn't it? Couldn't the universe be subtler?"

"Sometimes, you and others don't learn the lesson when it's subtle. Perhaps the universe had already given you feedback that you were being unkind to others and not being compassionate, but you ignored the warning. Progress happens in a spiral, not a straight line, and you spiral back again and again to learn different aspects and deeper layers of these and other positive qualities."

"Love, it seems to me, is the ultimate quality humanity needs. Why do I feel that love will solve all our problems?" I asked, puzzled.

"Love is reverence for all states and all beings, regardless of how others act or what happens. This non-attached, non-judgmental, unconditional love is the supreme reality and everyone must discover this."

"I've got a question and need some clarification."

"Go for it!" Henry replied.

"When I read books by people claiming to be self-realized, I have a fairly good idea if they are and, if so, approximately at what level by how they speak about consciousness. Of course, I realize that I'm incapable of assessing the consciousness of great masters as they are too far beyond me."

"So, what is the question?"

"I've read many books by the self-realized psychiatrist David Hawkins and have found them helpful in examining the progressive steps leading to merging with the Eternal."

"Interesting, but where are you going?"

"I've experienced higher states of consciousness than where I am now and wonder, if I'm regressing, or is there another explanation?" I replied. "Specifically, thirty years ago, I often experienced ecstasy in my bodies and the All-Being state that Hawkins says is a higher energy field than love— the quality I appear to be improving currently."

"I'm happy you brought up this point as it's important," Henry responded. "Thirty years ago, your sustainable vibration was lower than now, so you aren't regressing. At that time, you experienced occasional higher states of consciousness than your sustainable state, because consciousness is able to catapult individuals into a higher frequency for a short time, when either they've made exceptional progress in their present life or they're using a spiritual gift developed in another life. This happens more often the closer you come to enlightenment."

"And why is that?" I inquired.

"Because the closer you come to enlightenment, the more your soul infiltrates your personality, so that all lifetimes merge and all boundaries between physical, emotional and mental frequencies meld."

"These ecstatic episodes happened during the same years that I had what I refer to as 'fire attacks', which erupted as second degree burns all over my body. I knew that these burns were caused by the kundalini spiritual energy breaking through emotional blocks affecting my physical body and this went on for some years and then quieted. These ecstatic episodes were better than sex but, no matter how much I wanted to because my heart was immensely open, I could not facilitate bliss in others. I could induce ecstasy in myself, but resisted this to avoid potential addiction. Then these bliss times ended."

"Your knowing that it was important to refuse ecstasy comes from previous lives when you had a higher level of sustained consciousness than currently. In those lives, you realized that you must renounce ecstasy to go to even higher levels of consciousness and, in this life, you acted on this knowing."

"The problem is that I didn't go to a higher but to a lower state," I answered unhappily. "Furthermore, I wonder if this happens to others?"

"You did the correct thing as, at that time, you would have been unable to fully merge with the Eternal. It was not your destiny. Each person has an individual destiny in any given life, which seldom follows a straight line, and a person's destiny unfolds according to his or her soul's agreement. It was your destiny to fully explore all aspects of the ego and its emotional and mental games, in order to dissolve the ego while remaining in a physical body. Your journey has continually brought you to unconditional love, which you've been learning these last three decades."

"Good grief! I'm a slow learner."

"Not at all," Henry answered. "There are many ways to uncage your heart and you've been delving deeply into all of them. During this time, you became a step-mother and learned to put the children first, which is a mother's love. You entered a committed personal relationship where you learned forgiveness, gentleness and unconditional love."

"Correction," I interjected. "I have not fully learned these qualities. I'm still learning them."

"True, however celebrate progress. Also, during this time, you have given love and assistance to thousands in ways not even known to you consciously. Over time, you've uncovered deeper ways to uncage your heart and have realized the truth that what you do for others and for yourself is the same. The importance of uncaging your heart cannot be over-emphasized."

"Being a private person, I find this public display of my innermost secrets difficult."

"Letting people into your vulnerable areas furthers your path to release your identity, which is a requirement for conscious union with universal intelligence. Being willing to expose your wounds or secrets, in any way you feel you are hiding them, hastens the process. This is true for everyone, not only for you. There is a difference between telling your stories to increase your ego and sharing them to decrease the ego. You are doing the latter."

"Do you have any recommendations on additional ways to reduce the ego's influence?" I requested.

"Be alert and notice when you stray and then course correct. Continue doing what you are doing as it is an organic process."

"I have setbacks, but have noticed, when triggered, I stay in neutral–positive most often and do not relapse into old, negative behaviors."

"The ego wants to drag you into lower frequencies where it can control you more easily. To go forward, use willpower and continue to surrender all beliefs, roles, values, people and pleasantries to which you are attached. Remember you cannot earn enlightenment. Ultimately, it's a gift of grace."

"Are you saying that I and others may follow all the things you recommend and still not become self-realized? I don't think that's a great incentive to try, do you?"

"You make yourself attractive to universal intelligence through the methods we have been discussing. And you need to give up your attachment to being self-realized and deeply surrender everything to universal timing which you, in an ego state, can't know."

"Have we covered all the necessary positive qualities that will help?" I asked, somewhat mollified.

"Biological and electrochemical changes take place in the body when you experience positive, or negative, emotions caused by positive, or negative, life views and beliefs. These, in turn, either raise or lower your frequency that moves you either towards or away from self-realization. Tomorrow, we'll delve into the thoughtforms created by the ego to cage you and create your feelings of separation from the Infinite."

With those words, he ceased speaking.

Henry's feedback that I was successfully developing unconditional love—my number one goal—was heartening. I reflected on how we often notice a weakness, such as lack of compassion, faith or willpower, and commit to strengthening that quality, perhaps for years. During that time, it's natural to become discouraged with setbacks. Therefore, it's essential to celebrate our successes and stay optimistic that we are making progress— even if we don't become self-realized in this lifetime. I was reminded of a wonderful Chinese saying, "The secret of success is to fall down six times and get up seven." The journey to self-realization is a long-term commitment.

8

YOU ARE A HOLOGRAM

All that we are is the result of what we have thought.
The mind is everything. What we think, we become.

BUDDHA

The following day, I barely sat down and turned my attention inward when Henry launched into the topic that he wished to discuss. "Let me ask you a question," Henry asked. "Do you think the world is real?"

"No. I think it's an illusion," I asserted.

"And what is your proof?"

Henry's question triggered a memory of how I'd discovered that the world was an illusion. "Decades ago," I said, "I visited the Museum of Holography in New York City, which unfortunately closed in 1992. It exhibited life-size 3D holographic images of people in motion. At that time, I'd never heard of a hologram and was completely unprepared for the impact these images had on me. As I walked by the life-size moving images of a man riding a bicycle and a woman blowing me a kiss, I realized that all of us are illusionary holograms like those images, and that what we imagine to be our real world is a hologram too.

"This knowing was not theoretical; it was a door opening into another reality—somewhat like what must have happened to individuals 500 years ago, when they realized that the sun, not the earth, was the center of the solar system. When a paradigm shift like this occurs, you cannot go back to your earlier beliefs."

"And how has this 'knowing' changed you?" Henry asked.

"My revelation has inspired me to seek ways to show others that our physical world is an illusion. In workshops, for instance, I often ask people to touch the person next to them, while I ask, 'Are they solid?' Usually, people say that they are.

"Then I ask, 'What are they composed of?' Generally, I'm told water molecules.

"Then, I ask, 'What are water molecules made of?' To this question, they most often answer 'space' or 'ether'.

"To this reply, I ask, 'You know science has proven that everything is 99.9 percent ether, then why do you continue to see others and the world as solid?'

"By demonstrating the gap between what they believe in theory and what they perceive with their physical senses of sight and touch, I attempt to help them cross the bridge to perceiving the physical world as a hologram, an illusion."

"And have you been successful?"

"I don't know. Sometimes, we need to hear the same thing in different ways before our view of reality changes. I've watched scientific investigations into consciousness to see if, and when, mainstream science would encounter a similar paradigm shift to mine."

"And …?"

"I discovered that the quantum physicist David Bohm and neurophysiologist Karl Pribram began speaking of the holographic nature of the universe and of our brain about the same time as I had my knowing. Each of us experienced this paradigm shift through the filter of our particular area of expertise."

"This is not a coincidence," he replied. "When one person discovers something, he or she creates a thoughtform for others to follow. These thoughtforms grow stronger, as more individuals think similar thoughts. Each major thoughtform has various notes/tones/frequencies depending on the filter that an individual might use depending on their interests. For example, if you have a science filter, you will likely approach through a lens like quantum physics, mathematics, astronomy or neurophysiology. If you have a spiritual or mystical bias, your approach might be through meditation, spiritual books or commitment to a guru."

"Science is wonderful in the strides it's made in the last 50 years," I responded. "However, many mainstream scientific theories about our reality and the universe still conform to an ego-centered model."

"Universal intelligence," Henry commented, "is beyond the ego's vision and can only be experienced with a fundamental shift in consciousness that is not found in the 3D reality. Science has proof of the immensity of the physical universe, but is unable to make the leap to knowing the immensity of the intelligence that created it. You only have to reflect that the physical universe is made up of billions of galaxies that are made up of billions of solar systems that have billions of planets to imagine how great an intelligence would have to be to create it. And the astral and causal universes are much larger than the physical universe which astronomers see. The eternal consciousness orders all of this."

"Your example helps me to realize the immensity of universal intelligence but how does this impact humans? What steps must we take in our evolution to go from where we are now to re-uniting with this intelligence?"

"Presently," Henry replied, "humanity is at a crossroads. Humans have been hypnotized by the ego into believing that the physical world is real; humanity is now starting to see that it's an illusion. With this insight, humans realize that their thoughts have created their reality, which, in turn, means that with thought they can change their reality. Currently, the majority of people are applying this insight into changing only their physical reality to attract more goodies that their ego tells them will make them happy. Through creative visualizations, prayer, affirmations and notes on the fridge—all great techniques by the way—they draw money, assets and lovers to them.

"However, when they discover that gratifying ego needs still doesn't bring happiness, they'll ultimately turn their attention to freeing themselves from the ego's web. Increasingly, this is happening and, as more people free themselves, they create a wider path for others to follow. And they aren't alone. Universal intelligence is assisting in the process and its energy is permeating the causal and astral realms and trickling down into the physical."

"You've spoken about humanity's next stage in general terms but can you break it down into the steps we need to go through in order to become full creators?"

"Sure, if you think it will help."

"It will help me as I want to understand the steps I still need to take."

"Right now," he responded, "you and others are only conscious in the physical realm. You visit the astral realm in dreams and between incarnations but few of you are fully conscious there. You cannot stay in the astral realm until you are at a high enough frequency of consciousness that you no longer need to reincarnate in the physical world. Humanity is beginning to move to this stage currently. Even then, however, you aren't fully conscious and must reincarnate in the astral realm until you've released all negative feelings. Following this, you must remain in the causal realm until you've transmuted all negative thoughts. When you've done this, you unite with your soul and become one with universal consciousness."

"Correct me if I've misunderstood but aren't you helping me and others to clear our erroneous thoughts and feelings through your instructions? If so, aren't we clearing our astral and causal bodies while we're still in a physical body?"

"Well done! That is exactly what I'm doing."

"That's going to save some lifetimes, isn't it?"

"Only if you apply what I say. Agreeing in theory is not enough."

"What you're saying is complex," I said. "Paramahansa Yogananda puts it more simply. He says there are three levels of consciousness: The ego is both our ordinary conscious and subconscious, and the soul is the superconscious. Yogananda refers to the various levels of unconsciousness that we have been examining as the 'subconscious'. Some of these levels are closer to the surface and can be recalled from the subconscious with little effort. However, other levels are deeper and totally unconscious. For example, a person could have difficulty enjoying sex with her husband and recall quite easily, if she wishes, that this pattern existed with her other sexual partners. However, at deeper levels she may be unconscious that the origin of the problem stemmed from incestuous abuse by her father.

"I see these subconscious/unconscious, conscious and soul frequencies, which Yogananda speaks of, as permeating each other. And our soul in our waking day-to-day reality (what Yogananda refers to as the 'conscious' frequency) is no longer pure consciousness because it has become entangled with the ego. We are combinations in all three levels simultaneously.

"I'd like to ask a question. We've been speaking a great deal about the ego but could we discuss the soul for a change?"

"What do you want to know?"

"For a start, I'd like to check out my definition of what a soul is?"

"Which is …?"

"I regard the soul as an individualized reflection of universal consciousness. I believe there will come a time when our soul dissolves, leaving only universal consciousness that permeates everything. That will happen when we no longer need a personal identity. Is that correct?"

"The soul is necessary at a certain stage of human evolution," Henry answered. "Soul, or the superconscious, is an individualized level of consciousness. And, as you say, it dissolves when you no longer need it. The soul is in the realm of intuitive knowing beyond the mental realm of thinking. However, your journey doesn't end with the dissolving of the soul. There are many stages of enlightenment. Beyond soul consciousness is union with universal consciousness throughout all manifested worlds. This is sometimes referred to as Christ consciousness. And the final state of enlightenment is cosmic consciousness, which is union with the Infinite both within and beyond all creation. Buddha spoke about the final state."

"Obviously, I have a long way to go," I responded, not without humor.

"Strengthen your connection to your soul," Henry observed. "When you do this the soul gradually extricates itself from the ego. The ego cannot exist in that high a frequency and will dissolve when you move to that level of consciousness. To do this, let's return to our discussion of the negative and positive thoughtforms that exist in the astral and causal realms, shall we?"

"I have a question that's nagging me. If individuals are atheists who don't believe in the soul, will they be able to become enlightened?"

"When individuals practice compassion for others and all beings they move to the higher soul frequencies, regardless of their beliefs."

"Here we are back at love and compassion being the key for transformation. I'm happy for atheists but I must say I'm feeling frustrated that, although I practice most of your suggestions, a snail would progress faster than me."

"It may seem slow to you but you've chosen what's called the bodhisattva path. This means that you're committed to helping all beings, not only yourself, to awaken. When individuals are able to maintain a certain vibrational frequency of consciousness, they begin to raise the frequency of their family and the collective unconscious, at the same time as they increase their own."

Somewhat mollified, I asked, "Is there anything else you'd suggest to facilitate spiritual transformation?"

"Regular deep meditation is important. The ego doesn't exist in the higher soul frequency. By meditating deeply, you simultaneously raise your own frequency, that of your ancestral line, and the collective unconscious of humanity."

"Does meditation convert fear to particular qualities, like compassion?"

"As I've mentioned previously, every thought and feeling has a certain vibration. Therefore, it depends on your thoughts and feelings when meditating. Energy follows thought, which is powered by emotion, so decide what thoughts you wish and cultivate them."

"Does a feeling of gratitude towards a friend, or a teacher, need to be stronger than the fear of rejection, for example, for this to work?"

"What do you think?" Henry asked.

"I think that the positive emotion will gradually take over, as this is the path to consciousness. Yet, this could take ages, if fear is stronger than that of gratitude."

"That's the state of things. In that case, what could you do to strengthen the positive emotion?"

"I could observe my thoughts and, whenever they become negative, use willpower to change them to positive. Also, I need to remember all the wonderful things in my life. This would be more effective in meditation, as I'm already in a higher frequency, than during daily life. Better still, I could bring the neutral-positive approach into everything I do.

"Hold on! What if I'm already doing these things and feel that I'm not doing enough or not doing it right?" I asked, puzzled.

"Doubts about not doing enough and not doing it correctly are created by the ego," Henry responded. "These doubts are large, powerful thoughtforms in the collective unconsciousness of humanity. The great liberated teachers of the Vedas, the Rishis, called these thoughtforms sanskaras."

"Could you say more about how these powerful thoughtforms are created and how to dissolve them?"

"During the long period of humanity's evolution," he said, "individuals have discarded old ideas and beliefs as they've evolved. These old ideas create thoughtforms that, depending on their frequency, live in your physical, emotional or mental bodies. These thoughtforms carry an energy charge which body intelligences must continually program in your bodies, until you release the thought that created them."

"How do these thoughtforms relate to the ego?"

"The ego is the overriding thoughtform that uses the energy in these collective thoughtforms (sanskaras)."

"Could you give examples of these sanskaras?"

"Sanskaras are memories created over millennia by people thinking the same thoughts repeatedly and energizing them, either through desire—which is attachment, or repulsion—which is fear.

"Some relate to the mind and the mental body and are located around the head. These are religious and societal customs, commandments and high motivations of all kinds that have been replaced by higher ones. For example, earlier we spoke about how the Old Testament view of a vengeful God was replaced by a new view of a loving God in the New Testament. In the Aquarian Age this view will be replaced by the view that you are God."

"Your statement that I and others are God is going to be a leap for lots of people," I asserted. "I can imagine some folks will think that what you're saying is sacreligious."

"That's true," replied Henry, "because it takes hundreds, even thousands of years, for newer thoughtforms at a higher frequency to replace older ones."

"Are these spiritual and mental thoughtforms the main ones that we need to eliminate?"

"Not at all. There are negative, and even some positive thoughtforms concerning ideas and feelings, about personal value or worth that affect the emotional body. A case in point is feeling that you have to earn love by being generous and helpful. These thoughtforms generally congregate around both the head and heart."

"If some of the thoughtforms in the mental and emotional bodies are positive, as you say, why do they need to be eliminated?" I asked, confused.

"All thoughtforms are illusions. The ego clings to thoughtforms—even supposedly positive ones—in order to keep you under its control. You must eliminate all illusions. When you move to the soul frequency the illusion of separateness dissolves and you know that you have always been, are now, and always will be, one with universal consciousness."

"I see. You've mentioned thoughtforms clinging to the upper part of our body, are there any clinging to the lower part?"

"Around the mid-section of the body are more destructive feelings like hate, fear, anger, selfishness, possessive love, as well as many patterns making a person into a self-created martyr.

"And around the hips and lower back are thoughtforms affecting the etheric-physical body. They are of instinctive fears, such as self preservation, sex, self-assertion, and the belief that one is separate. Finally, around the feet are thoughtforms that prevent individuals from physically moving or acting."

"It's a miracle that I can move at all with all these sanskaras weighing me down," I complained. "I must say, the picture you paint doesn't sound hopeful. I didn't hear you mention any solutions in that long list of negative thoughtforms."

"Don't be impatient," Henry argued. "We're going to get to solutions when next we speak."

"Our conversation today has been heavy going and I'm full up," I said to Henry.

"I understand but it's important for you and others to see the long-range view of where you and humanity are going and how to get there. Speaking only about your personal life is limited. Sure, we can cover fears, negative beliefs and positive qualities you need to develop consciousness. However, I want you to see the larger picture of your full destiny and why doing the work we're doing is essential."

At that point in our conversation, I withdrew to consider what Henry had said. Reflecting on his definition of sanskaras—what I prefer to call thoughtforms—I was beginning to see that the ego was a kind of overarching thoughtform that used my minor thoughtforms to control me. I had a strong intuition that by recognizing the ego for what it was I was moving forward to free myself from it. I felt that my recognition contributed to the dissolution of the ego and allowed my personality vessel to hold more of my soul frequency. I looked forward to checking out my intuition with Henry when we spoke next.

9

THE NAUGHTY EGO

Turn your face to the sun and the shadows fall behind you.
MAORI PROVERB

For several days, I considered what Henry had not said, as well as what he had said. I was left wondering what my core *sanskara* (thoughtform) was. All roads led to the ego as the problem. It seemed to me that our conversation was circling in a kind of dance that gave me a feeling of progress, but which still avoided the core. It was clear that, until I did something about the core issue, it would be a weed continually growing in my garden of consciousness. But what could I do, that I wasn't already doing? Time to ask the expert.

"I have to understand my ego better. As the saying goes, 'Know your enemy,'" I said to him when next we spoke.

"That attitude is not going to get you anywhere," Henry replied curtly. "Thinking of the ego as your enemy is as much of an attachment as thinking of it as your friend. You need to view it objectively, in a neutral state, so that you don't give it energy. Energy of both repulsion and attraction feeds it."

"That's difficult to do when I know that it's holding me in illusion and blocking my path to consciousness. Is there any way you can help?"

"I can't eliminate the ego for you. Only you can do that, but I can discuss what the ego is so you will have a better sense of how it holds you in illusion."

"Go for it."

"Everything you think, feel, or do in your present life creates an energy footprint that will dictate the program of a future life. When you incarnate ego uses this energy to create the thoughtforms that control you. Moreover, because all thoughts, emotions, fears and desires are common to every human being, there is no such thing as a separate personality, ego, or 'me'. The ego is a conglomeration of many thoughtforms that hold your desires, wounds, life scripts that, in turn, create what you think of as you. However, there is no personal identity. You think you are unique, but your perceived differences from others are merely variations of the same thoughtforms used by the ego to program all humans. Wake up from the dream and free yourself from illusion."

"When I reflect on my present life, I feel like I am evolving in consciousness. If I am not unique, is my feeling of progress erroneous?" I asked, puzzled.

"In this illusionary reality, the reasons you evolve are your karma, willpower, devotion and positive attitude, which attract higher thoughtforms and strengthen your connection to your soul. But these higher thoughtforms are still illusionary. The ego cannot evolve beyond itself to awaken. The ego, the 'me', has evolved from your animal nature and is not the true Self, the eternal 'I'. The ego works with the brain and is limited in what it can, and cannot, perceive. The ego may be what you think of as your mind, or your mental body, but it also infiltrates your emotional and physical bodies. These three bodies are confined to the world of form and all form is illusion.

"The ego uses the senses of smell, touch, sight, hearing and taste to perceive the physical world. It feels and reacts to these senses with its emotions and either likes, or dislikes, what the senses perceive. Through the ego, the mind makes sense of its perceptions and takes a position based on its past experiences created by religion, family and environment. As part of animal man, the ego sees situations and others either as threats or desirable."

"Given that I'm listening to you with ego ears, I must be censoring everything you say according to my programming. How, then, can I free myself from its hold?" I interjected.

"You're already practicing many ways to do this. An inner space that feels like a pause in time exists between what is really occurring and the ego's interpretation of it. When you witness the ego's games from a neutral-positive, non-attached state, you lengthen the pause which gives you time to listen to your soul. Also, because the ego receives no energy when you are in neutral-positive, you lessen its power. The more you practice this technique, the weaker the ego becomes and the more you resonate in harmony with universal consciousness. Remember that the ego will do anything to maintain control and all its strategies are designed to ensure its survival. Some games are obvious, others are subtler, even not conscious for you. Gradually, as you become increasingly conscious, you learn to avoid the obvious ego games and most of your attention turns to uncovering the unconscious patterns."

"That's what I am doing presently, but it's a Gordian knot. Just when I think I have solved an erroneous pattern, another knot appears. Worst of all, I have no control over what is emerging or when. Sometimes I appear to make progress on an issue, only to grind to a standstill, or even regress."

"Wonderful!" Henry exclaimed. "That's progress. Surrendering to this transformational process is key, even if you aren't intellectually aware of what is happening. Trust this process and keep on track in allowing this."

"You can't imagine the temptations. I have urges to go to the toilet, eat food, bite my nails, drink coffee, answer the phone or emails, watch TV and have a nap. When I satisfy one urge, another one emerges. I'm aware that these are distractions and watch myself doing them. Mostly the distractions occur physically, but occasionally my emotions go up and down like a yoyo, from happiness to self-pity, for no apparent reason. It's as if the emotions are running all by themselves. Comments?"

"Do you feel guilty or depressed succumbing to the physical or emotional temptations?" he said, responding to my question with one of his own.

"Not usually. Sometimes I do what the ego wants and sometimes I deny it and watch how much discomfort I feel physically or emotionally. I'm experimenting with this presently. There doesn't seem to be a right or wrong approach, more like allowing and witnessing, when I'm doing, or not doing, what the ego wants."

"Have you considered being firmer and denying yourself what it wants?"

"I have but I don't feel this is the right approach at the moment, although it might be for someone else. As I'm so yang and strong-minded, I feel it's better to soften and become more yin. Is this correct or am I mistaken?"

"You can be yin and still say 'no' to the ego," he replied firmly. "Nevertheless, you are right that to work with the body intelligence efficiently, it's necessary to balance being and doing, yin and yang. These are the negative and positive polarities that create an electrical current in the body, which allows you to transform yourself. The modern world prefers doing, the yang quality, and is not nearly as keen on being, the yin quality. But it's essential to balance and practice both qualities equally. Too much yin or yang creates imbalance and tension, which leads to energy blockages in the physical, emotional and mental bodies. For your energy to flow in harmony with consciousness, it has to work equally with both qualities."

"By developing yin qualities, am I assisting my soul to eliminate the ego?"

"You are," Henry replied. "By allowing and surrendering to the trans-formational process, you break old patterns and attachments of being a certain way in order to be safe, loved, successful, and so on. This attitude breaks the ego's control. The ultimate attachment—not just for you but for everyone—is the fear of death and all the games of the ego are to ensure its survival. You don't need to destroy the ego like a samurai, or try to mentally outwit it, which wouldn't work in any case, because the ego is a product of your thoughts. You merely need to release your identification with it. Lead your life in love, develop deeper compassion for yourself and others, and surrender to the Eternal Source of all life. Doing this disempowers the ego. Understand that the ego-personality, like the physical body, is a useful tool to function in the 3D reality, but both are dissolved in the higher frequency of the soul.

"Don't force yourself to do anything. The ego loves a battle and the yang emotions of anger, pride and frustration will fuel it. Be persistent in adhering to your end goal of self-realization and practice the subtler, more yin, techniques to dissolve the ego. This will work in its own time. The power of love bypasses the mind and the greatest part of the ego's hold is in your thoughts."

"What do you mean by 'love'?" I inquired.

"The love I'm describing is universal love, loving every being, loving the Earth, and loving all wayshowers and saints who have gone before. You love all beings as yourself and yourself as all beings. See, feel and know that the source of this love is the Infinite, the Eternal Source. Loving all with devotion opens your heart and, as your love expands, your frequency increases. This higher love frequency bypasses the mental plane, where the ego-controlled thoughts reside."

"Could you give an example of an erroneous ego-created thought in the mental plane?"

"The most obvious is a belief in a heavenly state," Henry replied quickly. "Because the ego fears death, it has created an attachment to living beyond death in various versions of heaven. Depending on your religious beliefs, heaven could be dancing girls, angels, or bliss, but most are in different astral frequencies. The astral realm is where the various versions of heaven and hell exist that the ego creates as part of its illusion. This illusion begins, however, in the mental plane of the lower causal realm that you regard as your mind. But your mind, as I've said, is really your ego."

"I thought that the soul existed in the causal realm. How can the ego and soul be in the same place?" I asked, confused.

"The soul exists at a higher frequency in the causal realm, whereas the ego exists at a lower one. Remember, as the causal realm is part of the world of form, both will dissolve in a higher, future state. Freedom is going beyond having an individual self. Surrendering the idea of having your personal eternal soul is often the most difficult idea for spiritual seekers to accept."

"The idea of being a soul-infused personality has encouraged me on my spiritual journey," I interjected, not wanting to release 'my' idea.

"The key is the word 'personality', which is synonymous with ego. At a certain stage, the concept of having a soul-infused personality is helpful, but you've passed that stage now and must relinquish its hold."

"At the risk of appearing to be a whiner, what's left?" I asked.

"Being awake is difficult to conceive of from an unawake state, as it is beyond physical, emotional and mental definitions, although it includes all these."

"Vague. Very vague." I was not impressed.

"Okay. I'll try again. A butterfly is totally different from a caterpillar, and yet there would be no butterfly without the caterpillar stage. It's helpful to recall that the caterpillar digests itself in the cocoon to become the butterfly. The ego-dominated human is still in the caterpillar stage of evolution and must dissolve its former attachments and thoughtforms to become the awakened human."

"That's clearer but more detail is welcome."

"Do you remember about the stages of enlightenment that we spoke of in our last discussion? This is important—so I'll build on what we spoke of then." Henry paused and waited for my agreement.

I was not convinced that rehashing what he had said previously was going to help me better understand self-realization. However, I decided to withhold judgement to give Henry my full attention.

"The first stage," he began, going slowly, "called self-realization, enlightenment and awakening, occurs when you know that the physical world is a dream, an illusion, created by universal intelligence. This experience is not a theory to believe in, but your reality. Most individuals who claim to be 'enlightened' are in this stage. When you enter this stage you no longer need to reincarnate in physical form. However, you must still reincarnate in astral form, until all your emotions are in harmony with consciousness."

"Question?" I stopped him before he could continue.

"Can you be a bit self-realized but not fully?"

"Can you be a little bit pregnant?" he countered.

"Taking your example, what if you are nine months pregnant but you still haven't given birth? Isn't that a better way of viewing the difference between not being self-realized and being self-realized?"

"That's a good point and valid to some extent. Using your example, the evolutionary process towards self-realization takes countless reincarnations. As you come close to giving birth you experience the dark night of the soul. You leave the caterpillar stage and enter the cocoon where in digesting yourself, as we're doing together, you ready yourself to become a butterfly. The cocoon stage is the equivalent of being pregnant. The cocoon stage may actually transpire over a series of lifetimes where you do move slowly towards becoming a butterfly while still functioning in the world. During these lifetimes, you advance from being two months pregnant, to six to eight.

During this cocoon stage, you are partially a butterfly but still not ready to birth the new transformed being."

"Your explanation is helpful. It clarifies why sometimes I have breakthroughs into what I sense is self-realization but I don't stay there. I have glimpses of what self-realization is like. Say more about the astral realm as that is the next stage in our transformation."

"The astral realm," Henry continued, "is where you go in your dreams and between lives. There your thoughts and feelings create your reality faster than in your physical world. In the astral plane, you may see loved ones who have died and may even study with spiritual beings who are helping you to learn the lessons of that realm. As you learn these lessons, the effects carry over into your day-to-day life which catalyzes your transformation."

"Another question. So, even if I and others are not self-realized, we visit the astral realm?"

"When you are not self-realized the astral world is very vague and cloudy to you. It isn't your reality and you most often forget what you experienced there either when you awaken in the morning from sleep or reincarnate into another physical body. But when you become self-realized, you are conscious in the astral realm in much the same way you are conscious in the physical. The astral realm becomes your world until you clear all your negative emotions."

"But aren't your instructions helping me to clear my negative emotions right now? Isn't that what I would do in my astral incarnations after I become self-realized?"

"I'm helping you to clear your physical, astral and causal bodies now. The more we clear your astral and causal bodies now, the higher the state of self-realization you go to when you become self-realized because you don't have as much clearing to do in the astral and causal realms."

"This is fantastic. Is this the role of all body intelligences?"

"It is."

"So, working with you is the most efficient way to advance spiritually?"

"It's definitely one of the most efficient ways and this is why I often refer to myself as a body spirit. But we're still not finished with my explanation."

"Sorry, please continue."

"After you have completed your astral incarnations, you still need to reincarnate in the causal realm, until you have surrendered all self-identification as an individual. In the causal realm, your soul dissolves, as you no longer need any form. Then you merge with universal consciousness. These final astral and causal incarnations usually are much quicker than the incarnations in the physical, because the desire to be fully united with consciousness increases, as does the knowing when you are not united.

"Are you clear now?" Henry asked.

"You've done a super job clarifying the stages and I appreciate it. I understand everything you are saying theoretically but self-realization is still not easy to fully comprehend. I have read amazing stories written by and about awakened humans, yet I find it difficult to follow when they describe the awakened state. To be honest, it seems so elusive. At the risk of appearing stupid, what is the incentive to awaken?"

"The incentive is to avoid pain and suffering. The greater the pain, the greater the incentive to be free of it," Henry replied.

"Good point. Buddha said that the cause of all suffering is attachment to things of this illusionary world."

"You can't know about consciousness, you can only know consciousness," Henry replied. "However, if you hear or read words of self-realized beings, either in their physical or imagined presence, your frequency increases. This hastens your enlightenment."

"I'm fortunate to have been with self-realized people many times in my life. Although I recognize a presence in each of them as well as their unique gifts, there is one person whose very energy catapulted me into an altered state. His name was Franklin Merrell-Wolff. I met him in my 30s when he was in his 80s. I had never read anything about or by him and so the encounter was completely fresh without any expectations. Just being in his presence catapulted me into such a non-physical state that even speaking was beyond me. I was in Presence myself. From that experience I know how self-realized people catalyze others. However, I didn't stay in that state but returned to my ordinary physical reality after some hours."

"Awakening is a gift of grace by the Infinite," Henry said. "It happens spontaneously. Awakening may happen even in an unevolved personality. Some individuals, although this was not the case with Dr. Wolff, may even have what appear to be abrasive personalities but they are still awake."

"Are you saying that you cannot earn enlightenment?"

"That's it," he replied in a humorous tone. "Beings at a high level of consciousness can put others in enlightened states but usually others don't stay there unless it is their destiny. But you can make yourself attractive to universal intelligence through a combination of devotion and willpower. You are now and have always been one with universal consciousness, whether you are aware of it or not. Every thought has an energy charge that is observable at the sub-quantum level. Deep trust and surrender to the transformational process reduce the friction caused by fears that delay awakening."

"I must say," I interrupted Henry, "that this transformational process is physically, emotionally and mentally exhausting. Is this normal?"

"It is," he replied, not without compassion. "Contrary to what people might think, the path becomes more difficult the closer you come to freedom from the ego's illusion. In the last few physical lifetimes, every karmic pattern you have ever had returns as a memory to be released. If you don't do this, you are caught again in the wheel of reincarnation. Each time you rise to a higher state of consciousness, you attract its opposite lower state for you to refuse. These are personified as the temptations by Satan, which Jesus faced, and as Buddha's temptations by the demon Mara and his three daughters."

"Stop right there," I said. "There's something that's been niggling at me. I feel that we've been casting the ego as the bad guy as if it's the root cause of all our problems. Yet, if it's a thoughtform that will be dissolved when we become conscious, isn't there something above/beyond it that is the real source of our illusion and that has, in fact, created the ego? Is that the same force that Jesus called Satan?"

"You've put your finger on the central issue," answered Henry.

"Then, why the heck are we only getting to it now?" I retorted, frustrated.

"Because the answer to your question lies outside the realm of the ego and it's best that you discover this for yourself, as you have done, rather than to have me point it out. Furthermore, and it's a big 'FURTHERMORE', the entire topic of Satan tends to divide folks into two erroneous camps. The first is negating the force of evil as imaginary. The second error is being so terrified of this force that they want to climb into bed, pull the covers over their heads, and hope they'll not be seen and therefore will not have to deal with Satan."

"I get it! What we think of as evil personified seems too large, too impossible to think that little me, unlike Jesus or Buddha, could ever resist such a large force as Satan so that's why we've been talking exclusively about the ego."

"That's correct," said Henry. "Yet, of your own free will you have to stand firm against this force and, every time you do so, you move towards universal consciousness. As you resist the attractions and desires of the ego, you resist this overriding force of illusion. So, what we've been discussing is exactly what is needed."

"Nice! However, I'd like to focus on this larger issue for a moment as I'm now wondering, did humans create this great force that opposes universal consciousness and, if not, how did it come to exist?" I asked, wanting to go deeper.

"Now you've put your finger on the third reason that I was delaying speaking about Satan or Mara, but now is the right time and I'll answer your question. Universal consciousness, God, the Creator, as we've been discussing, is the source of everything."

I interrupted, "Are you hinting that God created what we think of as evil that, in turn, lured us out of Eden and union with the Divine? Why would the Creator do such a thing as it's led us to being mired in illusion, pain and suffering?"

"The answer lies with another paradox," Henry replied, before continuing, "and paradoxes are both/ands which are more difficult to embrace than the either/or way of thinking that exists in the ego-centered duality of the illusionary world. Although the Creator is Infinite and Absolute, he/she/it is also evolving. In its evolving state, this Great Being decided to create universes and to people them with beings that, although they were part of itself, could enjoy their own individuality. To do this, the Creator needed to cast over the creations an illusion of separateness, referred to as maya in the Vedas. This cosmic illusion was created so that beings could express their individuality and have free will so they could also become creators."

"I'm with you so far, but where does Satan come in?" I asked, intrigued.

"The intelligent force whose job it is to create this separation from universal consciousness is Satan or Mara," replied Henry.

"And how exactly is that evil? I think I might be missing something."

"Satan, who was an archangel, was entrapped in his own illusion and saw that if everything returned to universal consciousness, he would no longer exist so he wished to perpetuate the illusion of separateness. For every positive quality that the Creator made, Satan made a negative quality. However, his power is confined to the world of form so that when you resist the temptations of physical, astral and causal realms you return to union with divine consciousness."

"Thus, correct me if I'm wrong, Satan works through the ego to tempt us to stay in the illusionary world. You could say that the ego is a tool that is being used," I said, hoping that I'd put two and two together.

"Correct," replied Henry.

"I've a feeling that Satan is the prodigal son of the Bible, who leaves his father and yet, after much pain and hardship looking after swine, which could be us humans, he returns to his father. Is that true?"

"It is and Satan paradoxically is both the force of resistance to the Creator as well as part of the Creator. We're going to discuss more about illusions that impede consciousness tomorrow as I think that is plenty for today. Realize that you, like everyone, are self-realized, you just don't know it. But this is another topic and let's leave it for tomorrow."

Through our discussion my view of the ego had changed. It was no longer the BIG baddie hanging over me and standing in my way to enlightenment. Strangely, I didn't regard Satan or Mara in the light of a bad guy either. Somehow, all seemed to be confirming that the plan of the Creator was unfolding in the very way it was intended. Everything, whether naughty or nice viewed from these lower realms, was a child of the Creator. The ego and even Satan played a role in strengthening free will which was necessary for us to become a full Creator. In this illusionary world of duality where all was divided into good and bad I could see how these two forces existed in opposition, however in a higher realm beyond form all my dilemmas were resolving.

This meant that I still had more work to do. I looked forward to pursuing my discussion with Henry on higher aspects of truth and of paths through illusion to consciousness.

10

ELIMINATE ILLUSIONS AND WAKE UP

Will you, won't you, will you,
won't you, will you join the dance?
LEWIS CARROLL, *Alice in Wonderland*

Sitting down the next morning, before Henry could introduce a new topic, I said. "Our discussion yesterday about the role of cosmic illusion as an impediment to consciousness made me realize that I wanted to do an examination of the possible paths through this illusion. In Matthew Fox's book *Original Blessing*, he wrote about four paths to consciousness and I'd like to review these with you to see if I'm seeing my choices clearly. Would that be okay?"

"Of course, I'm interested to hear what you consider to be your choices and, most especially, your main path," he replied.

"For sure I'm not on the easy path," I asserted, before continuing. "The first path, Via Positiva, is rare, whereby individuals have little or no physical or psychological pain and still become conscious. Via Positiva reminds me of the Celtic myth of the quest for the Holy Grail—the Grail representing universal consciousness. In this legend Galahad, one of the characters, found the Grail quickly and with little difficulty. Wouldn't we all like that path? I think those folks skip the dark night altogether.

"A second path is Via Negativa, whereby one becomes conscious through a great deal of physical or psychological pain. This path reminds me of Eckhart Tolle who was a 29-year-old supervisor at Cambridge with suicidal urges, when he lost physical consciousness and woke up self-realized. Considering suicide is obviously a dark night and I'm happy this is not my path.

"The third path is Via Creativa, which often attracts poets, musicians and other artists. I find that path attractive, because it's more like play and you end up with a product, which appeals to my merchant mentality. Nevertheless, I realize that many artists undergo heart-wrenching experiences and the dark night of the soul in order to birth their art."

"That's three paths to consciousness you're not on, so what path are you on?" asked Henry, prodding me.

"The main path I seem to be on is the fourth one, Via Transformativa. This is Perceval's path in the Celtic myth of the quest for the Grail. Perceval had raw talent (gifts from his previous lives). Because of his spiritual development, he was able to find the Grail at an early age. However, as he lacked compassion, it disappeared and he spent years in the Wasteland fighting one battle after another (with his ego). Finally, he was defeated by his black half-brother (his unconscious shadow) who had compassion so he did not kill Perceval. When the conscious (Perceval) and unconscious (half-brother) unite in compassion, they find the Grail (unite with the soul)."

"The path of Via Transformativa is the most common," Henry interjected. "It's the path of evolution, which is a largely predictable spiral, with minor ups and downs, through a gradual ascent to consciousness over lifetimes. The Wasteland that Perceval encounters is an outer metaphor for the dark night of the soul where you are bereft of inner meaning."

"Back to the myth," I said, "Are you my unconscious, the black half-brother, who is uniting with my conscious state to help me unite with my soul? I find that the more we discuss, the more this question arises for me."

"I'll attempt to answer your question but it is too limited as to my function. You love to put me and life in boxes and sometimes things cannot be boxed.

"On one level, you could say that I represent the unconscious that is re-uniting with your conscious state. In that way you could say that one of my aspects is what Carl Jung calls your 'shadow'. Your 'shadow' comprises aspects of yourself that the ego does not want you to recognize as they do not fit with the self-identity the ego is perpetuating which you mostly regard as negative aspects, such as jealousy, wanting to be the center of attention or wanting to win. But I may also be aspects of your unconscious that are brighter and more beautiful parts of yourself than what you are prepared to acknowledge for fear of being egoistic."

"Wow! You're right. I assumed that my unconscious was all negative things about myself. Is this a common problem for others?"

"Absolutely," Henry replied. "Your ego doesn't want you to merge with your unconscious because when you do, it loses its control of you. For this reason, it has you think of your unconscious aspects as scary or bad."

"This is an immensely freeing idea," I replied, grateful.

"With every advance in consciousness," Henry continued, "you trigger a reaction from the astral world of its opposite. In this way, Perceval drew to himself his opponents, which were aspects of his shadow. For example, when your energy rises to a higher frequency, you may become challenging to others, so you may be fired from a job unjustly, or spouses and friends may leave you for no apparent reason. These unwelcome challenges are opportunities to release all attachments, so you can rise to an even higher state and be free from ego control. There is immense power in the unconscious and when you surrender to it (as Perceval did with his half-brother) you become authentic and are no longer controlled by society's roles and values. I, your body spirit, am helping with this.

"In the face of all challenges, have compassion for yourself and others, just as Perceval's half-brother had for him. Through this approach, your unconscious merges with the conscious and together they merge with the soul, the superconscious."

During these many talks with Henry, a question grew, "Who was he/she/it?" Perhaps it was my ego wanting to define and even take ownership of him. Perhaps, on the other hand, it was my soul, my higher self, that wanted to trust what he said, so as to continue on the path I had been taking for so many years.

At the risk of 'boxing' him, I asked, "Are you a construct like the ego or the soul, or are you another aspect of universal consciousness?"

"You can determine the answer yourself," he replied, amused.

"You have access to all memories of my lives so that rules out the ego, not to mention that you are helping me to eliminate the ego. That leaves the soul. But the soul, as we discussed previously, is not the ultimate level of consciousness and, therefore, is a construct, like the ego. So, we are back to the same question, 'Are you a construct?'"

"Puzzle out your own answer," he prodded.

"You call yourself a body elemental, body intelligence, or body spirit and you said that you exist between my physical incarnations, at which time you are united with all body spirits. I know that you exist in the astral and causal realms because you build the physical, astral (emotional) and causal (mental) bodies. I'm not attracted to mysteries. I'd rather have an answer."

"Have you examined all possibilities?" Henry suggested, pointing me in another direction.

"There is universal consciousness and it's in all forms, which would include the ego as well as the soul, and this consciousness is present after physical death. Although I can see that consciousness is in you, as it is in the constructs of the ego and soul, I don't know if you are only consciousness. Universal consciousness is also in both my conscious and subconscious/shadow states of which you stated you were a part. I'm puzzled!"

"What part of consciousness sets down into physical, emotional and mental forms?" he nudged.

"I think of consciousness in form as being the active intelligence of wisdom. In many traditions, this intelligence that has created all form in each individual, our planet, solar system, and entire universe is represented as the Divine Mother, which is the same as the Holy Spirit in the Christian tradition. Are you saying that you are that?" I asked anxiously.

"Ask yourself: Why does this 'possibility' cause anxiety?"

Not wanting to answer his question, I countered with, "If you were the Divine Mother, why didn't you call yourself Henrietta or Sally?"

"I kind of like the name Henry and, besides, why do you think the Mother needs to be female? That is a limited view. Active intelligence is neither masculine, nor feminine. It encompasses both aspects. I chose the name Henry instead of a female name to jog you out of one of your old paradigms."

"You asked me why thinking of you as the Divine Mother caused me anxiety and we both know the answer. If that is the case, I would feel unworthy, inadequate and pressured to take what you say 'very' seriously. Also, because my listening is partially influenced by my ego, I might be incorrect and mislead others as well as myself."

"I hope you realize that your feelings stem from ego doubts and old programs," Henry asserted. "It's important to examine what is occurring for you as it is a common problem for many people. There is a difference in frequency when you say 'universal consciousness' or 'active intelligence' and 'Holy Spirit' or 'Divine Mother'. Your attachment to a spiritual thoughtform causes you to elevate the Holy Spirit and Divine Mother into an exalted idea that is above you. In contrast, you lessen universal consciousness and active intelligence by confining them to more mental, scientific terms. I want to make it clear that it's not the words you are using, but your feeling for the words. Spirit, Divine Mother, Christ Consciousness, Universal Consciousness and whether in form or formless—need I go on—are ONE. You need to feel this in your heart, mind and cells of your body."

"I've always felt close to Spirit," I replied, considering the truth of his assessment. "Perhaps because of the mystical experiences I've had since an early age. In fact, my first contact with the Infinite was through Spirit. The second was through the Christ and only then did I begin to open my heart to the Divine Mother. A feeling for the Divine Father still eludes me."

"How individuals view aspects of the Infinite evolves as they do," Henry interjected. "Although all aspects are One, some individuals feel more comfortable with a male God, like Jehovah. Others with the Divine Mother aspect, and some with the child Jesus. Still others are more comfortable with the Infinite in its formless aspect, such as Brahman of the Hindu religion."

"I agree with everything you're saying, but can we return to exactly what a body intelligence is?" I asked, not wanting to lose this opportunity to define him.

"A body intelligence is consciousness in form. That's why I often refer to myself as a body elemental because I'm composed of elements of the physical world of form. Universal consciousness, in its aspect as the Divine Mother, which is the same as the Holy Spirit, creates all form in all worlds and universes. Think of me as the Spirit that creates your bodies. I am body spirit which is synonymous with the active intelligence of universal consciousness."

"You stated previously that, when you formed my body in its first incarnation, you had no free will and developed free will as I evolved. If you are the equivalent of the Holy Spirit or Divine Mother, how could you, a godlike being, not have had free will?" I queried, still not ready to accept his revelation.

"Spirit forgets itself in form. Even the soul is dulled as it descends into matter and enters the personality. This is the story of the fall of Adam and Eve whose actions resulted in their removal from Eden, the state of union with consciousness. As the soul throws off the ego and ascends again, both you and I remember who we are. For you and most others, this remembrance is gradual."

At this point Henry paused to give me a moment to reflect on all he had said. "I want to discuss the major illusions that keep you and others in separation from universal consciousness however, before I do, I want to ask if you are clear on what I am and do?"

"I admit that even though you gave me clues throughout our discussions about who or what you really were, I've been thinking of Spirit and my body intelligence as different. I thought Spirit was an aspect of consciousness that gave me bliss and took me out of my body, and that my body intelligence was a lower being that I could program to be physically healthy."

"Oh. A kind of slave," Henry replied. "This ego-centered view has led humans to want to control and use the natural world, because they think of nature as being different from and less than Spirit."

"Hold on. I feel falsely accused. I've taught that nature and Spirit are one for years. For me the issue hasn't been that nature and Spirit are different but that nature and I are. I thought of nature as being 'out there' but didn't think of nature as being 'in here' in my physical, emotional and mental bodies. In some way, I kept nature and me separate."

"This separation is created by the ego that sees itself as a separate entity," Henry said. "This is the central illusion that must be dissolved. Everything we have discussed until now leads to this illusion. Remember, humans originally chose to separate from consciousness and to individualize, which created the ego. The ego lives in the core wound of your body. This wound can be seen as the feeling of separation, abandonment, or not being loved which is the central issue for most people. The Eternal Source did not create this wound, humans did. The ego, this false self, the me, is the core illusion that creates all other illusions."

"My patience is wearing thin," I exclaimed. "I've worked on everything you've suggested including eliminating my fears, healing life scripts, correcting negative beliefs and even practicing positive qualities to promote consciousness. And through it all I've attempted to maintain a neutral-positive attitude. And now you say we are FINALLY getting to the core issue. I'm frustrated and exhausted by this seemingly never-ending journey to self-realization."

"I hope you realize your ego is speaking," Henry replied without pity. "It's becoming more and more anxious with your progress and is bringing out the big guns. We should have covered patience under positive qualities. I think we missed it."

I remained quiet and attempted to re-establish my equilibrium.

"Transiting the dark night is a very painful process if you identify with the ego. You feel as if you are cut off from others, the Eternal Source and from your inner self. You no longer know what to believe or what to do. Although this stage on the spiritual journey feels empty it's actually progress. The less you cling to your self-identify, which is the ego, the easier it goes. You are ready to leave the ego-centered values behind and are going through the transformation to be a self-realized human. This is the next stage in your evolution and currently there are many people going through this transformational process. This path leads to union with all life.

"Self-realized humans," Henry continued, "experience no separation from all beings, including animals, plants and minerals. They use the personality vessel to work in the world to fulfill Spirit's purpose, but they have no personal goals. That said, they may still have preferences, however without attachment. Also, in higher states they even lose these preferences. Through awareness, self-realized people attract to themselves the circumstances and people that lead to fulfilling Spirit's purpose."

"I can relate to everything you're saying." I agreed. "You've convinced me that separation from the Eternal Source and clinging to my self-identity is the central issue. However, when you have a very large problem, which is what the ego is, I've found that it helps to bite off smaller chunks to deal with it. Therefore, could you speak of some smaller illusions the ego creates that I still need to remove? I attempt to eliminate any illusions I spot but perhaps I've missed some."

"I will discuss the main illusions, but believing they are false in theory is not enough, you must act to eliminate them in everyday life. Here goes. You cannot own anything. This includes but is not limited to money, possessions, children, spouses, pets. Any attachment to these is based on a feeling of possession that they are yours. How are you doing?"

"Room for improvement," I answered, "but I've got my feet to the fire in these areas."

"The second illusion is that all the senses, including taste, touch, hearing, smell and sight, give accurate descriptions of what is real. And that appeasing them will give you happiness. Any comments?"

"Only that speaking with you has at least tripled the amount of time I fantasize about appeasing my senses. Our discussions cause my ego a great deal of anxiety so it gives me visions of eating chocolate, having naps, and much else. I'm attempting to squelch these desires as I know they don't give ultimate happiness."

"Trying to detach from the senses makes the ego feel that it is about to die, causing the ego to panic," Henry replied. "Use firm willpower to resist its urges and witness how much force it uses to create these urges in you. This brings me to the next illusion.

"You can't earn enlightenment by being good. Consciousness has no concept of being fair or that you can earn a reward. Consciousness is beyond good or bad definitions and asks you to get beyond these too."

"Destroying that illusion is difficult for me," I commented. "I was a 'good' child, in order to be safe and loved by my parents. This good behavior carried over into my adult life and brought me many rewards. People liked me and I was successful. Therefore, something in me still believes that if I'm 'good' by working hard and applying all the techniques you recommend that I'll become self-realized."

"The solution," he interjected, "is to do what I recommend for its intrinsic benefit without any expectation of a future reward."

"Actually," I answered, "the more I live in the present and work when I want, doing only what appeals, the less concerned I am about a future reward, even enlightenment. Thanks for the reminder. I needed it."

"Now, I want to discuss a more difficult illusion for spiritual people. The thinking mind, as it is part of the ego, cannot know reality. It creates its own version of reality. For example, humans have created human-like images and hierarchies of angels, gods and goddesses to represent consciousness. Consciousness is not individualized."

"But, in the world of form, these beings exist as individuals, don't they?"

"They do in the world of form. But, ultimately, all belief in forms, even those of a spiritual nature, is erroneous. You must surrender your physical, emotional and mental bodies that I built for you, as well as your identity, all of which are illusions. This is how Spirit is freed from the form world."

"You don't make self-realization sound attractive," I said, hoping I could retire to the couch for a nap.

"That's what the ego thinks, for sure," Henry replied, amused. "We've been examining illusion; now let's consider what is real. Consciousness is independent of time and place. There is no here, there, past or future. Everything is present now. There are changing states in consciousness, even as ice, water and water vapor change states, but are made of the same components. Consciousness becomes increasingly subtle in higher states and expanding your consciousness continually requires relinquishing a lower one."

"What is the best approach to reach these higher, more subtle states?" I asked.

"Meditation helps to create more inner space between thoughts, feelings and actions. This inner space, which is like a long pause, disarms the ego because the ego receives no energy."

"I have blank periods, like you are describing, not only in meditation but during the day. I may be walking in nature, taking a shower, or having a cat nap. Many inspirations come then."

"Great. During those blank periods you are united with consciousness in being. The more you meditate the more you will increase being."

"What is the best way to meditate?"

"There are many techniques. Zen and insight meditation help to increase inner space and being. But I'd like to recommend something to add regardless of what meditation technique you use. Meditate with devotion and love for all beings, while asking for assistance from spiritual avatars who have gone before—be these Christ, Buddha, Divine Mother, Archangel Michael, or your embodied spiritual teacher, if this person is self-realized.

These beings are one with universal consciousness. For instance, Jesus was an individual in the physical world and in union with consciousness as the Christ. Individuals who have reached a high level of consciousness, such as Krishna, Tara, Mahavatar Babaji and Buddha, are in the same stream with Christ. By praying with devotion to great avatars you draw their energy to you to transmute your lower frequencies. This is one of the powers of meditation and prayer."

"I understand how important meditation is. However, could we examine some other strategies that I've used to eliminate the ego and its illusions?" I asked.

"Go on then!" Henry responded.

"One of my big illusions is that I have to earn love and the way to do it is by being good and perfect. I want to give up this illusion as I believe in my soul that the Infinite loves me unconditionally and that it is okay to make mistakes. So, when I behave in a less than ideal way, I take steps in self-forgiveness. For example, I remind myself that I'm not perfect but am progressing, which helps to eliminate feelings of guilt or disappointment in myself. Sometimes, I admit my failure to others and ask them for forgiveness. On occasion, I even joke about my failings and point them out, even if others haven't noticed. These strategies lessen, even neutralize, my self-attachment to being good or perfect."

"Do these behaviors work?"

"I thought you'd tell me, but if you ask me, they do," I replied.

"How do you evaluate your progress?"

"I forgive myself faster and easier if I fall short of being perfect. This increases my energy and self-worth. Also, I've observed progress in situations where I would have been negatively triggered previously. Now I have more patience with others and myself as I no longer feel that they or I need to be perfect. I've learned to embrace even difficult situations as opportunities to grow. I am loving myself more."

"It's often easier for people to love and forgive others than themselves."

"That is certainly my scenario and I have been uncovering reasons why I don't love myself fully and how this came about. Previously, we discussed family scripts. In addition, I've found it helpful to examine the stories I tell about myself both in public and to myself. I've changed them, from being

unfairly treated or suffering to accepting 'what is' and to pointing (
positive outcomes from these situations. I feel that I'm eliminating negative
and self-limiting scripts this way."

"Your ideas are excellent and I suggest another exercise. Make a list
of all the ways in which you are loved. This will help you to focus on the
positive and to embrace all the love coming to you. This will help eliminate
your illusion that you are not loved unconditionally."

"Whoa, I completely missed doing this," I answered. "Now I see that,
by only eliminating the negative, I may not be open to receiving as much
love as the universe wants to give me. For instance, I might be pushing
away people who love me."

"The tendency to work on removing negatives, before adding positives,
is due to a lack of self-worth. This behavior is common to many. It's part of
the collective human thoughtform stemming from cutting themselves off
from the ever-present love of universal consciousness."

"Listening to you, I perceive another self-sabotage, which is not asking
fully for what I want. This stems from feeling that I don't deserve the best
and, if I have more, maybe someone else would have less. In this way, the
ego creates pain because I never receive what I want. This is the result of
scarcity mentality, isn't it?"

"A good insight," Henry said. "To correct this problem, I recommend
praying and affirming totally what your best-case scenario would be. Then,
completely release attachment to receiving what you've asked for, so the
universe can decide what is best."

"Even considering asking for what I really want creates anxiety. This
thought triggers fear of disappointment that I won't receive it, which, in turn,
would affirm that I'm not loved 'enough'. It's easier for me to stay in a neutral,
non-attached state than to stay open to unlimited abundance. Obviously, it
would be good to immediately put your suggestion into practice."

"Speaking of loving yourself, this is a BIG topic and let's continue with
it tomorrow. Over and out."

Something deep inside me relaxed knowing that Henry, or should I say
Henrietta or the Divine Mother, was Spirit. Thinking of him as body spirit
felt comforting and inspiring at the same time. I felt more fully embraced
and unconditionally loved.

I mulled over what Henry had told me and made a list of all the ways I was loved. It extended beyond individuals to include deep gratitude for my entire life. I loved my work, health, beauty in nature, and even difficult situations that had given me opportunities for growth for which I was grateful. Through these examples and many others, I felt loved by the universe and in alignment with it. Feelings of more or less, and disappointments in what I hadn't done, or things I hadn't received, no longer bothered me in the same way they might have previously. I felt a calm contentment. Doing and being merged and I felt no pressure to finish anything but to enjoy the unfolding journey.

11

LOVE HEALS YOUR CORE WOUND

*I do not expect anything from others, so their actions
cannot be in opposition to wishes of mine.*

SWAMI SRI YUKTESWAR, as quoted by
Paramahansa Yogananda in *Autobiography of a Yogi*

Days passed until I was ready to speak again with Henry as I lived within
a peaceful flow of being and doing.

"Have you noticed that underneath this calm there is still anxiety?"
Henry asked, waving aside my progress.

"I have but I'm not paying attention to it and am focusing on the
positive state," I replied.

"The underlying anxiety is the ego becoming increasingly worried that
it's losing control."

"I'm aware of that and this is why I'm not recognizing its anxiety. I
know I'm not that anxiety and am relaxing into the love and peace that is
universal consciousness."

"Wise approach," he responded. "The more you cultivate love and peace,
the stronger they become, until they are your permanent states. To move
from a fear-based life to a love-based life, it's necessary to love everything
because everything is an aspect of the One."

"You gave me an assignment that I've been practicing," I said, hoping
for feedback. "It was to ask for something I'd like and to remain in neutral
as to whether I'd receive it. I've noticed that, with this attitude, unfulfilled
wishes either didn't bother me at all or only minimally."

"Have you practiced asking for something you really want, as I recall
that is difficult for you?"

"A few times I've visualized something I really want," I answered. "I find this more difficult because I question if it is the best thing for me to have. Surely universal intelligence knows what is best, so shouldn't I accept what I'm given? I have a feeling I'm missing something with these conflicting thoughts, but I'm not sure what it is."

"You are caught between a spiritual law and a self-limiting life script," Henry replied. "It's common for spiritually-oriented individuals to do this to themselves. The self-limiting script is a version of scarcity thinking: you can never have everything you want and to ask for this is to be greedy, which is not spiritual. It's true that the Infinite knows what is best for you but, as you have free will, it wants you to ask. When you ask for what you want, it will decide what, how, and when to give it to you. Not asking is a problem and not feeling you deserve it will undermine your request as will any negative thought."

"Are you recommending to trust that my requests are for the highest good of myself and others?"

"Remember," he replied, "the Infinite is synonymous with boundless love. Even as parents want to give their children everything for happiness, the Infinite wants this for all its children. Ask for what you think your soul wants your personality to have; however, your top priority, above all else, must be union with the Infinite. Not from an ego perspective, as something to achieve, but from soul yearning to be one with the Infinite."

"Can this soul desire come from an inner knowing that I was originally in union with consciousness and that it was the most wonderful state of all-encompassing love and that I will inevitably return to this state?"

"This attitude will assist your progress. However, be aware that the ego wants to claim ownership of this belief and will cause you to be lazy in its pursuit. It's essential to maintain a humble attitude and realize you are entering an unknown place where surrender is the only option. You must continually commit to the process."

"The more I let go, the more expanded and relaxed I feel, and the more my tolerance and patience increase for others and myself."

"You will come to a stage," Henry offered, "where you have no judgment and then words disappear."

"I already have words disappearing but I thought this could be either age, or the result of a concussion some years ago. Even earlier, and for many years, I've encountered blank periods where neither thoughts, nor words come to me."

"Being without thoughts or words occurs when you are no longer in the mental realm, which is under the control of the ego. These blank periods and inability to find words are transitional states that will pass. After self-realization, you will no longer need words, unless it's your destiny to continue needing them."

"I've noticed that my teaching has changed. Formerly, I created lesson plans and researched my talks and workshops so I was totally prepared. Then, when I began teaching, I relaxed the plan and embraced the people and situations that arose. I regarded this practice as a both/and balance between thinking and feeling, wisdom and love. Now, I'm almost resistant to making lesson plans. Instead, prior to giving keynote talks, I ask for Spirit's help to fully open my heart to give others what they most need. Doing this, I feel immense love radiating through my heart and the words that are needed flow effortlessly. Others have responded well, so I'm continuing with this practice. However, I confess that a slight concern about failure descends as the numbers of listeners increase."

"Do you face the fear and let go of your notes even when there are large numbers?" he asked, helping me to go deeper to find the cause of my problem.

"I think it's the same problem you diagnosed before. I trust my heart and the universe when there are small and medium numbers of people (say 200). However, with large numbers (say 1000), I want the notes there for support. This is a version of self-limitation and lack of trust in the universe, isn't it?"

"Yes! I'm happy to give suggestions. Are you ready?" Henry asked, sensing my approval and then proceeding. "You withhold, depending on the day, between 5 and 15 percent of what you think of as 'yourself' from surrender to the ever present, all loving Eternal Source. You know surrender is necessary, but you don't remember the wound that makes this difficult. The original core wound is separation from the Eternal Source which humans chose themselves. The symptoms of this wound may take different forms in each person and include fears of abandonment, failure, change, the unknown, and other fears. Everyone has a core wound they protect but, ultimately, they must expose it for it to heal."

"The minute you spoke of an unremembered wound," I responded, "I saw myself in three different situations being thrust unwillingly into a public spotlight and forgetting the words I was supposed to say. Forgetting my lines was the symptom of an underlying belief that, because I wasn't perfect, I would fail and then be rejected. I think this is how my core wound manifested and each successive occasion of forgetting my lines was in front of more people.

"The third time it happened I was eighteen, just starting university, when I was asked by the dean of Victoria College at the University of Toronto to accompany Dr. Northrop Frye, considered one of the world's greatest literary critics, in welcoming all the first-year students. It was impossible for me to refuse, despite my immense fear, for the dean had made my speaking a condition of being allowed into residence, as my marks did not qualify.

"I rehearsed the words that the dean wanted me to say and the day came. Dr. Frye, his wife and I were having lunch prior to the ceremony and he was so introverted that he was having difficulty talking to an eighteen-year-old. I found myself introducing topics of conversation to put him at ease. This situation gave me the comforting insight that, if this brilliant, albeit introverted man could speak in front of so many people, surely I could too. And did I do well? Not exactly. I forgot the dean's lines, so the pattern of not remembering others' words hadn't changed, but when it happened, I spoke from my heart and the words flowed. That was when I first learned to trust the universe to give me the words that wanted to be said."

"Isn't that what you said you are doing now? How is that different from before?" he asked.

"I seem to manage better in a crisis when I don't have time to censor myself. If I'm totally out of my comfort zone with no safe place to anchor, I surrender and do my best, which means to be who I really am, my authentic self, perhaps even my soul. Yet, when I'm asked to speak as the expert on a topic, I tend to be more mental and speak from what I know, rather than who I am."

"Have you noticed inner changes?"

"The more loving I am with others, the more I am with myself.

Whenever I am in new situations now, I have little anxiety because I trust that the best thing for all concerned will happen. This could be in my work, such as teaching and writing, but also in wounded and fearful inner areas of which only you and I are aware. It feels as if the clouds, the miasmas, are clearing and only wisps of old patterns and erroneous scripts cling to me."

"You are not overstating what is happening. You tend to understate your progress, as you don't want to be prideful. Understating and overstating one's progress are both inappropriate. Your inner compass is aligned to the end goal and the goal is pulling you forward as much as you are yearning for it. Yearn more, will you!"

"You make me laugh. Another story comes to mind. May I?"

Henry gave me an inner nudge to go ahead.

"I sometimes feel that I lack devotion. A year ago, I was wondering how to become more devout and mentioned this to an enlightened guru friend. Prajnaparamita was amused by my question and said, 'You are devoted. Look at your dedication for 20 years to the International Institute for Transformation that you founded.'

"Her comment caught me by surprise and I replied, 'I think of devotion as being a yin quality, being softer and more yielding than I am. I want to be more yin and devoted in that sense.'

"'A spiritual teacher wields both a sword and a flower,' Prajnaparamita answered.

"Her recontextualizing 'devotion' helped me to remove any judgment I had about myself as lacking something. I could still maintain the goal of becoming more yin without feeling that I lacked devotion." I was reflecting on the difference between being yin and being devoted when Henry interrupted my reverie."

"Devotion fuels your soul," he said. "Because you love the Eternal Source, you love all beings created by it, and love yourself as you love all beings. The key for self-realization is unconditional love."

"Your comment reminds me," I replied, "of something else that happened recently that also shattered my old self-image. For years, I've had the goal of being more loving to everyone and in all situations. During my birthday party this year, the universe reflected back my own self-judgment about not being loving enough. The party organizer invited my students and friends, who knew me from all areas of my life, to share what they appreciated most about me. I was ready to hear about my dedication to serve, wisdom and good humor, but each person, without exception, commented on how loving I was. My old self-concept shattered with the realization I was love and didn't need to prove it any longer. It was a beautiful moment that has strengthened me in self-love ever since."

In speaking about that loving time, love flooded me again and Henry gave me time to feel this before he commented. "When you feel love, appreciation, compassion and gratitude, endorphins flood your brain and body, resulting in more happiness. Unconditional love increases love for both self and others, because you have neither expectation from them nor need of anything for yourself. The ego is disarmed and negative thoughtforms fade."

"I've noticed that the more loving I am, the less anxiety I have, even if circumstances facing me are more difficult. I feel blessed that I'm flowing in the current of consciousness. I haven't yet merged with it but I feel, with increased ease, the ego shell dissolving."

"Love and positive feelings literally stretch and relax your DNA," Henry commented. "Conversely, feelings of fear, frustration, jealousy and anger contract it making you susceptible to illness and disease. The DNA responds to both your attitude and approach to challenges in daily life, so your energy and frequency rises or falls depending on your choices. There is a split second between something occurring and your interpretation of it. If you maintain a neutral-positive awareness, you will not be triggered by the ups and downs of events. As a result, your thoughts and feelings will not cause the release of stress hormones. Instead, I will be free to keep your emotions and endocrine system stable and healthy."

I started to interrupt, but Henry stopped me. "Let me continue. Your inner and outer life are linked in a feedback loop. The more you create a calm, peaceful and loving inner life—which, by the way, is facilitated by meditation—the more your outer life reflects these qualities and vice versa. Willpower and persistence are needed to stabilize your emotions, so that your ego cannot control you by adrenaline rushes fueled by negative emotions. In this way, I'm able to heal your adrenals and bodily system."

"Your recommendations are great in most situations," I commented, "however sometimes we might be in a very difficult situation where we can't think of a good outcome no matter what we choose to do."

"If," Henry replied, "you cannot immediately enter a peaceful, loving state by changing your thoughts, then, rather than dwelling in a negative state, raise your endorphins through exercise, walking in nature, taking a break, and visiting upbeat friends. Get your mind off the distressing issue and return to it later, when you have insights about either how to change it positively or, if you cannot, to accept the situation."

"Is there a possibility of becoming attached to being loving?" I inquired. "Wouldn't the ego try something like that?"

"The ego will do anything to increase the feeling of 'me' and 'mine'. The key to becoming unconditionally loving is not needing acknowledgement from others for loving, generous acts, as this feeling creates attachment. Instead, allow love to flow through everything you do, so you are love. Surrender everything to the Infinite and, when you do, compassion grows and flows through you and synchronicities, joy, peace and inner happiness abound."

"Is there anything else to focus on during the return journey to consciousness?" I asked.

"Qualities that are under- or over-developed are different for each person and are dependent on the state that the individual creates through thoughts," answered Henry.

"Could you mention some of these? I'd find it helpful to reflect on where I've been, where I am now, and what I need to avoid and practice in future."

He paused before answering as if he was considering how best to be helpful. "We've already discussed this previously," he said finally. "One of the ego's tricks is to keep you wanting more information, as if awakening were a puzzle to solve but you will never have all the pieces. At some point, you have to get off the mental merry-go-round and say 'Enough!' It's best to contemplate what we've discussed today."

For many days after we spoke, I reflected on love and areas in which shadows still existed, while simultaneously celebrating my increased lovingness. I felt kinder towards myself and did not blame or punish myself for errors. Meanwhile, my commitment to universal consciousness increased, which, in turn, led to greater happiness. Roles and responsibilities no longer seemed anchored to 'shoulds' and felt fluid as I lived life authentically.

I observed that the present stretched, as I lived more fully in it, and I increasingly wanted to live in it. By living in the present, old ways of being and anxieties lessened. As the inner space between my thoughts and feelings increased, I realized that my anxiety was often linked directly to a negative thought. For example, noticing that I was living more in the present was followed by an anxiety of not having enough time to do what needed to be done. This anxiety led to a realization that the ego was matching my positive feelings with negative ones in an effort to undermine me.

Now, however, since discovering the ego was only a tool of the intelligent force of illusion, it seemed to have shrunk to a manageable size. I began thinking of the ego as a naughty child who only wants its own way and a solution on how to deal with it emerged without effort. I discovered that, if I felt gratitude for universal guidance and had awareness of universal love, it weakened the ego and the force of illusion behind it. Also, if my body occasionally flooded with anxiety, I could dissolve the tension by taking a deep breath and releasing it fully.

I realized increasingly that sharing my current spiritual journey with others might help them on theirs. Previously, I had always waited until I was certain of the right answers before sharing my thoughts with others. This was another old pattern that I wished to break as fears of failure and rejection were attached to it. By writing and speaking about my ongoing journey, I committed to trusting the universe more deeply.

12

HOW THE ETHERIC BODY FEEDS THE PHYSICAL BODY

In the province of the mind, what one believes to be true either
is true or becomes true within certain limits. ...When found,
these limits turn out to be further beliefs to be transcended.

JOHN LILLY MD

More days passed and I remained in a neutral state with no expectations or resistance. Finally, one morning I turned my attention inward towards Henry to find out if there was something else he wished to discuss.

"Yes," he said, picking up on my thoughts. "Your physical body, as I hope you understand by now, is a whole system. Each cell is intelligent and communicates with other organs and bodily functions."

"Our examination of what was needed to establish health by correcting erroneous thoughts and feelings was so thorough that I had almost forgotten to focus on the physical."

"That's not a bad thing," Henry replied, "because physical illness and disease begin in the mental and emotional bodies. Nevertheless, today we will focus on the physical. Before discussing some physical organs, it's essential to examine how I work through the etheric body to maintain the physical body.

"There are three etheric channels that I use to convey life-giving energy to all your organs. These etheric channels meet in each of the seven chakras and I work with thousands of *nadis*, made up of arteries, veins, and so on, to feed your physical, emotional and mental bodies. The literal meaning of 'nadi' is flow and *nadis* are channels for the flow of consciousness. Just as the positive and negative forces of electricity flow through complex circuits,

3 MAIN CHANNELS & CHAKRAS

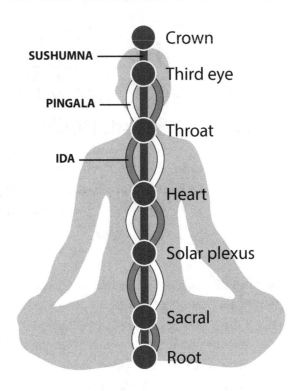

in the same way, *prana* (life force) and *manas* (mental force) flow through every part of your body via these *nadis*."

"Is it necessary to be so technical? Can't you explain what you do simply?"

"I'm using Hindu terms because western science, as yet, has learned very little about etheric physiology. Body spirits are etheric beings that work with the physical body and I'll simplify how I function to give you a firm foundation of understanding. Amongst these *nadis*, three channels are the most important. The central channel is the medullar *sushumna*. It interpenetrates the cerebrospinal axis from the perineum to the juncture of the lamboid and sagittal suture at the crown of your head. It extends from the base chakra to the crown chakra. The *sushumna* is the central channel and the kundalini circulates in it when you are awakened.

This happens when the energy from the right and left channels, on either side of the central channel, are balanced and then they merge and move up the central channel. This occurs when you are able to magnetize and balance your yang and yin energies so that etherically a high frequency current is established."

"Is this the main reason it is important to balance the yin and yang energies that we spoke of previously?" I asked. "So that it's possible to establish a current to go up the central channel?"

"It is," Henry answered. "The channel on the right side has a positive polarity and is associated with yang qualities of active mental states. The channel on the left side has a negative polarity and is associated with yin qualities and passive mental states. These two channels cross at all chakras and merge in the third eye.

"The various positive thought and emotional techniques, which we've been discussing, purify and develop energetic currents in these two channels. This process, working in conjunction with the heart, leads to awakening. When the heart maintains a coherent rhythm through maintaining positive emotions, your entire vibration increases, leading to consciousness. We will speak of this more when we discuss the heart."

"This is a heck of a lot of information. Is it all important or can we talk solely about the heart and brain?" I inquired.

"I'm telling you not only the work I do but also how I do it. If you understand better the 'how', you can understand the importance of adhering to positive thoughts, feelings and actions that create health. I use these three etheric channels to connect and work with the physiological heart, brain, organs and cells. To free yourself from the thoughtforms and illusions that control you, it's helpful to understand the etheric and physiological workings of these organs that will help you to do this."

"Although Western science," I commented, "may lag behind in their knowledge of the etheric body, they have physiological evidence about the effect of emotions on the brain. For example, Dr. Richard Davidson at the University of Wisconsin studied electrical brain activity and blood flow to map out the areas of the brain that reflect positive and negative emotions. He discovered that the left prefrontal cortex is activated by positive emotions, whereas the right prefrontal cortex is activated by negative emotions. Davidson conducted experiments on highly trained contemplatives, meditators, and those who have made inner development their top priority. He discovered that their levels of activation of the left prefrontal cortex, the site correlating with positive emotions, was way beyond those of non-meditators. Because the mind, like the body, is trainable, his study shows that anyone can change their brain through meditation. Yet, what I don't understand is how does changing the brain lead to higher states of consciousness?"

"To answer your question, we need to look at the pineal gland," Henry said, eager to help me understand. "The pineal gland is located between the two cerebral hemispheres in the very middle of the brain. It is the size of a grain of rice and shaped like a pinecone from which its name derives. (See pineal gland illustration on page 8.)

"The ancient Greeks thought the pineal gland was the seat of the soul and it does play a strong role in consciousness. It's coded and programmed by universal intelligence to help you to evolve into a conscious being. Jesus said, 'The light of the body is the eye: if therefore thine eye be single, thy whole body shall be full of light.' These words mean that higher light frequencies enter the pineal gland, also referred to as the third eye, as a single beam of light. This single beam of light is composed of three different etheric rays of energy. These rays are the same as the three flames of love, wisdom and will within your heart."

"The self-realized guru, Paramahansa Yogananda," I interrupted, "also speaks about these three rays of energy and their effect on the brain. He says that the ray of God the Father (path of will) is found predominantly in the white matter of the brain, which is located inside the brain and insulated from the exterior grey matter. The ray of God the Son (the path of love) is found predominantly in the grey matter of the exterior brain, which provides the medium through which thoughts might be expressed. The ray of the Holy Spirit (the path of wisdom)—that's you, Henry—is found predominantly in the red blood cells and manifested as the electrical current that flows through the nerves."

"Yogananda is correct," Henry commented. "He describes what happens etherically. And, ideally, my function is to balance these three rays of energy in your physical, emotional and mental bodies. Still, as you have free will, my functioning is controlled by your thoughts. This is why we have been focusing our talks on eliminating negative and strengthening positive thoughts. Every time your thoughts align coherently in a higher frequency, I can signal the pineal gland to open codes of thinking that previously were inaccessible to you. These higher thoughts create higher feelings that facilitate your spiritual transformation."

"While we're on the topic of the pineal, there are a few other things I'd like to check out with you. Is that okay?"

"I'm waiting …"

"For many years, I've been studying the function of the pineal gland," I said. "I've felt, as you've confirmed, that the pineal is the key to unlocking higher states of consciousness. I've learned that the pineal gland contains two kinds of crystals. The larger ones are mulberry-shaped and the second ones are minute and have been referred to as myeloconia (Greek for brain dust). These myeloconia are geometrically-shaped calcite crystals that may very well have piezoelectric properties which means that they could generate an electrical charge. If so, it means they have the ability to increase our energy vibration. For such a small organ, it employs a great deal of blood—second only to the kidneys and equal to the pituitary. As you are Spirit flowing in my blood, Henry, this information tells me that you visit the pineal gland a great deal. Is that true?"

"Yes, it's true," he laughed. "As you might know, the pineal gland is not connected to the brain and only has nerves connecting it to the autonomic nervous system. The pineal gland is, in many ways, the link between the etheric and physical bodies. The pineal gland is connected etherically to the sixth chakra—the third eye. That is where the positive and negative side channels terminate and merge with the *sushumna*—the central channel that has a neutral charge. When you maintain a positive state—one of devotion and will to know God—I can use the electrical current moving up your central channel to activate higher states of consciousness, which are encoded in the pineal gland."

"Thanks for explaining how you work with the pineal. Is there anything I and others can do physically to strengthen our pineal gland?"

"Cleaning and detoxifying your pineal gland are important as that strengthens its connection with universal intelligence. Fluoride is detrimental to the pineal and it unfortunately absorbs fluoride more than any other organ. So, if possible, don't use fluoride in your tap water or toothpaste."

"Eliminating fluoride is one thing, but is there anything we could add?"

"You'll be happy to hear that raw cacao is a pineal stimulant and an antioxidant, so eating it can be helpful. Chocolate is known to cause the production of endorphins that make you feel loved and this emotion, as with all positive emotions, strengthens the pineal gland."

"No wonder I love chocolate so much!" I exclaimed, excited at the possibility of increasing my intake. I was thinking that our conversation about the brain had ended and was leaving to get a few of those endorphin and pineal enhancers … when Henry commented.

"Our discussion on the physiological and etheric functions of the brain is not just for you. Others, who will read this information, will benefit. Many individuals need scientific proof before they will believe what we say. We've focused on the importance of thoughts and feelings and now we give proof to ground our assertions."

At that moment I became aware that this information was heavy going. I LOVE discussing the correlations between spiritual literature and what biological science is discovering about the workings of the brain. However, I sometimes forget that this topic has been a passion of mine for years and that I might overwhelm you, the reader, with my backlog of 'fascinating' information that I'd like to share. So let's take a breather and come back later.

13

THE BRAIN:
DEVELOP YOUR SMARTS

*A great many people think they are thinking
when they are merely rearranging their prejudices.*

DAVID BOHM

Henry was ready to continue when I sat down to chat with him again.

"We've discussed the pineal gland, but I'd like to broaden our discussion to the importance of the entire brain because, as Yogananda rightly said, the entire brain is involved in housing the three rays of universal consciousness."

"If you want to discuss the entire brain, could I share what I've found out about *glial cells*? I've found it very interesting and others might too."

"Go for it!"

"Glial cells," I began, "make up 90 percent of the brain cells. They support and surround every nerve fiber in the body and increase synaptic connections. In fact, unlike neurons, glial cells increase throughout our life if we continually learn new things. Our environment can increase, or decrease, the number of glial cells in our brains and the pineal gland is composed of a great number of glial cells. When Einstein's brain was investigated, it was found that he had 72 percent more glial cells than the average person. Because Einstein, in addition to being a genius, was also a mystic, I've wondered if having more glial cells may assist in spiritual transformation?"

"Glial cells grow or shrink," Henry replied, "depending on the frequencies of the information you give them. They grow when you increase your love, and intellectual or spiritual pursuits. For example, your glial cells and intelligence have grown throughout your life and I'll explain how.

When you started secondary school, based on the results of your IQ tests, you were placed in a class for those of average intelligence. You were not interested—and not good may I add—in some subjects offered, such as secretarial and home economics. So you studied hard in the academic subjects to be able to enter the academic stream the next year.

"However," Henry continued, "your vision only extended as far as finishing secondary school. It was your destiny to attract friends who were going to university, to open you to that as an option for you too. Once again, you initially limited yourself by taking the shortest, easiest possible degree, but the universe intervened and you finished with three degrees. Throughout your life, you have expanded your glial cells by continually learning and this is what everyone can do."

"Your comment reminds me of findings by a neuroscientist, Michael Merzenich, who discovered that the brain has a plastic quality and is molded by experience. As we learn new skills, new pathways open up. Even older people, who keep mentally active, have more complex brains than ones who aren't.

"On a personal note, I've often wondered why my original IQ scores were not very good and I think I know the answer. Studies at Baylor Medical School revealed that children who are rarely touched or stimulated develop brains that are 20 to 30 percent smaller than average. As a child, my physical, psychological and mental environment was not very stimulating, which could account for a lower IQ score when I was young."

Henry was chomping at the bit to comment. "Touch, and mental and emotional stimulation are essential for all-round health. And not only for children. Even seniors do better if they are touched and given interesting environments. I can't over-state its importance."

"Just speaking about how I 'supposedly' became smarter gave me another insight. The educational system when I went to school focused more on left-brain rote learning. The teacher verbally told you information that you were asked to remember. This didn't work for me as auditory is my least developed learning style. I was unable, until later in university, to use my right-brain intuitive gifts, which are more visual and at a higher frequency."

"Many children don't succeed in traditional educational institutions," interjected Henry, "because they don't have an auditory learning style.

Fortunately, this is changing and schools are beginning to accommodate diverse ways of learning. Science has discovered that the brain continues to develop in significant ways into a person's 20s and even later. Humanity is evolving towards learning styles that involve whole-brain integration that occurs faster than the speed of light. This is becoming evident now and will be provable by science shortly."

"Whole brain thinking that's faster than the speed of light! Your words support what Dr. Karl Pribram of Stanford University Medical School has discovered. Dr. Pribram's research shows that the brain works like a hologram. One small part of the brain has access to all the information that is stored in other parts. As a result, when one part is damaged, another part, through training, can replicate the missing function, although it doesn't do it in exactly the same way. It's through this hologram that we create our reality, which evolves and changes as we think differently."

"True," Henry commented, smiling. "Your reality changes as you change your thoughts and beliefs. Humanity is entering an era when science is venturing into territory known previously only to mystics. This knowledge will change your world as humanity moves from its present state of ego consciousness to global consciousness and to the transcendent consciousness of the soul."

"Is this the global consciousness that Maharishi, the founder of Transcendental Meditation (TM), was referring to when he mentioned that one percent of the people meditating would help the entire world to become conscious?"

"Maharishi was correct," Henry answered. "You can produce coherent thought patterns by meditating regularly. When you do this, you are able to unify data throughout your brain, allowing reason and emotion to communicate together in both your mind and body. This may produce new paradigms of thinking and consciousness."

"The scientific term for what you are describing is synchronous oscillation," I added. "Science has discovered that 40 hertz is the frequency at which synchronous unitive thinking occurs and this frequency is more often found in meditators. This unitive thinking characterizes individuals who have a visionary, higher mind. Unitive thinking allows them to do more creative, intuitive and rule-breaking thinking. Also, synchronous oscillation integrates the mind, heart and soul and this integration, in turn, leads to quantum jumps in consciousness."

"It's a wonderful time in human evolution," Henry agreed, "when science is discovering why meditation is important. Meditating regularly accelerates spiritual transformation. In fact, it eases your way through the cocoon stage of the dark night, especially in the earlier and middle stages. During the final stage of emptiness all spiritual practices, such as meditation, prayer, reading spiritual books, might fall away … but that is another topic."

"Speaking about the importance of meditation, Andrew Newberg, a neuroscientist at the University of Pennsylvania and the author of *How God Changes Your Brain,* has discovered fascinating things about the effects of meditation on the brain. He has taken brain image scans of Franciscan nuns, Buddhists, Pentecostals, Sikhs and Sufis as they pray or meditate, all in his quest to map the effects of spirituality on the brain. He states that there's not just one 'God' part of the brain. He's found that when you fully engage the mind, which typically happens in spiritual practices, it activates various parts of the brain. Thinking of 'God' in a positive way, turns on the part of the brain that makes you feel more compassionate, loving, forgiving of others and ourselves. It also lowers your levels of depression and anxiety.

"Newberg also found," I continued, "that many different meditative techniques have the same effect. And it doesn't take a lot of time to gain benefits. He took people, who had never meditated, scanned their brains and then trained them in simple meditative techniques. The individuals meditated for 12 minutes a day. At eight weeks, Newberg saw significant improvement in memory and emotional measures, including anxiety, anger and tension. Furthermore, it appears that these results are cumulative: the more you meditate, the greater these positive results are.

"Henry, I could quote scientific research until the cows come home but I'm aware that my frame of reference is limited by my ego. You are the builder of my body. From your etheric point of view why is meditation important?"

"Meditation," Henry responded, "allows me to use the nerves and etheric chakras of your body to connect your physical and etheric nervous systems. These physical and etheric systems have two functions. The first is to connect you to the world. The second is to connect you to universal consciousness. The life force (*prana*) ordinarily flows from universal consciousness to the brain, spine and nerves to activate your physical senses and connect you to the outer world. However, during meditation, the energy flow is reversed to flow inward. When this happens, universal consciousness feeds and develops the chakras and more subtle bodies, to prepare you to move to higher spiritual frequencies.

"Therefore, it's essential not to overexcite your nerves through overwork or worry, and to maintain an inner and outer calm. Such an attitude nurtures the nerves. Otherwise, you burn the sheath surrounding the nerves with too much energy and do great damage. Meditation is necessary to help me maintain equilibrium in your anxiety-producing world. Retreats and even walking in nature daily are also very soothing. Talking too much, too much activity, or stimulation through entertainment, such as films and television, can also overexcite the nerves."

"Talking too much, you say. I feel we've been doing that," I said, hoping to end our conversation.

"One last thing," Henry replied.

I conveyed my fatigue but he continued anyway.

"The spinal column protects the kundalini energy that must rise from the base to the crown chakra. It is important to carry yourself erect with the skull aligned atop a straight spine. This allows the energy to flow from the pineal gland into all of the chakras so that its universal connection becomes a living part of your bodies. When this occurs, consciousness in the higher mind becomes body consciousness.

"Our discussion about the brain has been thorough," he paused, before concluding, "and we still must speak about the second major organ of consciousness in the body—the heart. But this is a big topic so let's leave it for tomorrow."

I was full, actually overfull of information, but I recognized the importance of what Henry and I had discussed about the brain. I was struck by how science was now discovering and proving what many spiritual teachings purported. Intuitively I felt that, with both ways of viewing reality agreeing and supporting each other, humanity was entering a time for a quantum leap in consciousness to take place. A time when we would move beyond focusing on the functioning of physical organs, such as the brain, and science would discover that the field of consciousness—of which the mind is a part—is where healing on every level takes place.

It was clear that to increase our intelligence, we need stimulation by continuing to learn new things mentally, emotionally and physically and by using all our physical senses. Simultaneously we need to meditate to allow our learnings to integrate and to integrate and balance the left and right brains, leading to whole-brain synchronous thinking.

14

UNCAGE YOUR HEART

*Perfect consciousness can accept the soul, whose
dimensions are infinitely small ... Located in the heart,
it distributes its energy to the whole body.*

MUKANA UPANISHAD

Days came and went before I was ready to sit down again with Henry. I
felt incapable of knowing all that might be said about the importance of the
heart. Perhaps, as the heart has always been associated with love, it felt more
intensely personal than the brain. I reminisced that, six years earlier, when I
was first writing this book, I called it *Uncage Your Heart*. I felt then, as I still
feel now, that uncaging the heart was central to my transformation and that
of others. Just as I had not been able to continue writing about the process
then, thoughts about tackling the topic now were daunting.

One day, buoyed with chocolate, I turned on the computer and
telepathically called Henry.

"Chocolate raises your endorphins so that you feel loved," he began,
picking up on my current interest. "That's why many people crave chocolate.
So now that you feel loved, let's talk about the heart as an important key
to spiritual transformation. When individuals live in fear, they have a cage
around their hearts that protects them from others and stressors in their
environment. But the cage does not eliminate fear and only by eliminating
the armor will they become fearless. There are only two ways to live: in fear
or in love. Fear is the way of the old era that is passing, and love is the way
of the new one that is beginning.

"The love of which I speak," Henry continued, "is not only the love
of your children, parents, friends, but also loving everyone and everything

equally. It's the love of the higher heart—the etheric heart. Buddha pointed the way to the etheric heart when he said, 'Love everyone as you love your mother.' Jesus the Christ did the same when he said, 'Do unto others as you would have them do onto you.' In the Hindu tradition, unconditional love is called 'royal giving' and it's the highest form of love."

"This may be an odd question but where is the etheric heart located?"

"Would you believe in the ethers?" Henry laughed. "Every physical organ, even every cell, has an etheric counterpart. When you and others correct the cause and not only the symptoms of a physical problem, you correct the damaged etheric organ. This is why we are devoting so much time discussing the thoughts that cause physical, emotional, mental and spiritual illness."

"If we're talking about the etheric heart as being the higher aspect of love," I commented, "I feel that the Hawaiian word *aloha* points the way. Aloha is made up of two words. The first '*alo*' means the bosom and the center of the universe and '*ha*' means the Divine breath. When you have aloha, there is no boundary between you and the other, or between your personality and soul. You live what Jesus and Buddha taught. For example, to act with *aloha* for Hawaiians means to invite strangers into their home and to feed the spirit within them, as well as their physical bodies."

Henry jumped in. "Aloha is a great example of loving with the etheric heart. Hawaiians, like most indigenous peoples, know that all is interconnected and what affects one affects all. As your frequency ascends to your etheric heart, you will live this principle, not solely in theory but in everyday reality. Loving others fully is connected to loving yourself fully, which is connected to loving the Creator of everything fully. Your etheric heart also mediates between your personality and soul. By uncaging your heart, you open to consciousness without boundaries and interconnection with all existence. Thereby, you become a true guardian of the Earth and live in peaceful harmony with all creation."

"As with the brain," I remarked, "I've researched how the heart affects consciousness and have discovered evidence of which I was unaware. I think this information supports what we are discussing. For example, the Institute of HeartMath in California has proven that the electromagnetic field of our hearts is up to 60 times stronger than that of the brain.

The field extends at least twelve feet from the heart and is so powerful that an electrocardiogram reading can be taken three feet from the body. Furthermore, the heart is intelligent. It reads the emotional state of others, regardless of what others say or do, and signals the rest of the body how to feel about that person and whether someone is trustworthy or not.

"Besides this, they have discovered that a person's heart frequency influences not only someone nearby, whom they know, but also strangers in another location. This could explain how people intuitively know if a loved one has had an accident or died. Likewise, it might indicate why so many individuals knew something terrible had occurred when the Twin Towers were hit in New York or when hurricanes and other disasters have happened. Presently, our planet is beset by numerous wars, health and environmental crises, and refugees fleeing their homes. Is it possible that these events cause a never-ending level of anxiety in people around the globe? Do their hearts sense these tragedies even if they have none of these problems in their personal lives?"

"Absolutely," he agreed. "The good news is that, because people around the world feel this floating anxiety, they are moved to do something about it. People begin to meditate, do yoga, read self-help and spiritual books drawn from all traditions, become environmental activists, and bring refugees to their hometowns."

I agreed with Henry's positive ideas but decided to offer a balanced viewpoint. I said, "These positive steps people are taking lead to consciousness, but I'm concerned about the long-term effects of ongoing anxiety that adults feel, which they pass on to their unborn children. For instance, studies show that the embryo's electromagnetic field resonates with that of the mother in utero and that her emotional state affects the brain development of the child. Cellular biologist Dr. Bruce Lipton has even proven that the DNA of the unborn child can be affected by the mother's positive and negative emotions. If the mother is fearful, she programs fear into her child."

"No-one exists in isolation," Henry explained. "As I continually remind you, all is interconnected, not just in this present life but in past and future lives. Both gifts and wounds that a child inherits are there because of his or her karma, the choice of parents and the time the child incarnates.

All is there to be healed, and healing can happen at any age for both parents and children. Healing starts in the heart."

"What you say may be true," I interjected, "however, healing is not a simple process."

"Is that so?" he said, not sounding convinced.

Obviously, Henry needed more proof from a human perspective. "For example," I began, eager to oblige him, "studies have shown that the degree of unconditional love children receive during the first three years of life profoundly affects the functioning of their heart and brain for life. Also, we know that at age 11 or 12, just before the growth spurt of puberty, the brain, under the direction of the heart, undergoes a spring-cleaning of useless neural connections. If children feel safe and loved, the brain will focus on new growth and possibilities. Conversely, if children feel unsafe and unloved, the brain will focus on retaining survival information. This choice determines how the prefrontal cortex of the brain will develop. Even if children feel loved by their parents, it's easy to understand that, when their parents feel continual anxiety, their children feel the same way."

"I prefer to focus on the glass half-full," Henry responded. "Children have free will, even at age 11 or 12, to decide which of their parent's beliefs they will, or will not, adopt. By that age, they have interacted with other children, adults and other sources that can alter their thinking. Each child has his or her own karma and destiny. Some children have difficult parents and thrive, while others have nurturing, enriching environments and flounder."

I had to grant that his point was accurate. I could think of many examples of where some children excel in difficult environments and others wither. I postponed judgment and waited for Henry to continue.

"Humans often don't change their behavior until they have proof for why it is important to change. Now, as you mention, scientific proof is available and entering mainstream consciousness to support the effectiveness of positive thoughts at any age. When you eliminate negative mental and emotional states and generate positive ones, I, as your body elemental, your body spirit, am able to uncage your heart so you can access the higher soul frequency. And people have free will to decide to change at any age."

"I'm relieved to hear this and I'm sure others will be too," I volunteered, mellowing my position. "Actually, the Institute of HeartMath, has done research that substantiates this claim. They found that, when we feel positive emotional states of love, compassion, care and appreciation, our hearts enter a sustained rhythm that they refer to as emotional coherence. This coherent heart pattern leads to increased synchronization and entrainment between multiple body systems that, in turn, lead to optimal health and performance. What I found especially interesting in their findings is that we can 'intentionally' create these positive feelings through visualization and breathing techniques and, by doing this, our hearts become emotionally coherent too."

"Negative emotions, such as anger, anxiety and fear," Henry said, "cause me to desynchronize your heart rhythms, which makes it difficult to regulate your emotions. The key is to generate positive emotions by visualization, meditation, prayer and contemplating what you appreciate in life. You could say that meditation is more yin, prayer more yang, and contemplation more neutral as you witness what is, without attempting to change anything. I prefer you to generate peaceful, neutral-positive, unconditionally loving emotions, such as gratitude, rather than elevated excitement which is more yang. Doing this allows me to create a coherent heart rhythm to maintain health in all your body systems."

"You mention prayer," I commented. "We've spoken so often about meditation that I feel prayer has taken a backseat. I think meditation and prayer complement each other. When you pray, you often ask universal intelligence for something, whereas meditation is listening to what it says to you. To me, both prayer and meditation open your heart and both can help on the path to consciousness."

"Prayer," Henry agreed, "is as important as meditation. The two work best in tandem and sometimes you or others emphasize one over the other."

"So let's discuss prayer in more detail," I commented. "Medical doctor Larry Dossey has written extensively about the effects of prayer. Studies have been conducted whereby individuals prayed for patients they did not know who had undergone heart surgeries. The patients who were prayed for did significantly better than those who were not prayed for. They had fewer deaths and recovered faster. Furthermore, it made no difference if the prayers were by a Christian, Jew or Hindu, etc.; it was the positive effect of prayer that was important."

"In a busy life," Henry replied, "it's easy to fill your day with activity and not take time to meditate, pray and contemplate beauty in the world. Some people might also feel guilty that they are not doing enough for the Earth or for others. Neither overwork nor guilt benefit you or others. By meditating and praying daily for others, yourself and the Earth, you make a positive difference in the world as well as achieving greater peace for yourself. Meditation and prayer are energetically balanced, as you mention with your telephone metaphor, and doing both allows me to keep your body healthy."

"I have a confession. Lately, I've felt increasingly empty," I said. "Not in a bad way but I no longer want to meditate, do visualizations, read spiritual books or 'work' at becoming something other than what I am. Sometimes thoughts that I'm being lazy or not doing enough cross my mind but the most important thing seems to allow what is happening to happen. Nothing in me wants to push forward or quicken the process even though I'm aware that others would prefer that I functioned and produced as I have in the past. And yet at a very deep level I'm continually saying, 'Thank you' to the Divine. I'm not resisting the process. Is this progress or regression?"

"This is progress when it comes naturally as it has come for you: when you can remain in a neutral-positive contemplative state even if your ego attempts to trigger something in you. This time marks the dissolving of boundaries that separate you from the Source of all."

"Will I ever want to meditate again?"

"Meditation, prayer and all active spiritual practices are things that you have done to get to this stage. They can take you no further at this moment. Now you need to be open to receive Spirit's plan for you. These practices may return or not. Stay where you are and continue to say 'Yes', and to welcome the Source of all with open arms. That is all you have to do and all else will come in its own time. Grace is outside time. There is nothing more important for every individual than to surrender to the conditions of their present moment and listen to Spirit. In doing so, you serve the whole."

"It feels a bit like dying and I've even wondered sometimes if I'm going to die?"

"The ego is dying and all you can do is to stay attentive and welcome the process. There are no specific actions to take or not take. You can't figure out the process intellectually so it feels as if you are losing control."

"I do feel like that. I've even wondered if I'm getting senile dementia as I can't function as effectively as I used to. I'm slower and less perfect. Still, all this feels okay. In fact, and this will sound strange, I feel a kind of happiness that I'm letting this happen and that it is happening. Let's say, there's a sense of rightness and gratitude and I want to say how much gratitude I feel for all your help with this process, Henry."

"You are increasingly in more subtle states. Being and doing, and the outer and inner worlds are merging."

"Is this part of uncaging my heart?"

"It most certainly is and, as you continue to surrender and welcome the process, without qualifying it, your physical body becomes more filled with *prana* and returns to health."

"Could you be more specific about how you use *prana* to keep the physical body healthy?"

"We've been discussing the heart, but its effectiveness depends, to some extent, on the condition of the lungs," Henry answered. "Both the heart and lungs are affected by emotion and both deteriorate with fear. When afraid, you don't breathe properly and your heart beats too quickly and wears out. Learning to slow your heartbeat through deep breathing, which is practiced in most meditation traditions, is important. When you do this, I'm able to completely oxygenate your heart and circulate full, not partial, nourishment throughout the body. As your lungs breathe more deeply and your heart beat slows, I have more vitality and love to distribute to the rest of the body. Once your heart is calm, fear decreases significantly. Another benefit of deep breathing meditation is that you live longer because there is not as much wear on the heart."

"Previously we discussed the fact that you, as my body consciousness, live in my blood. What are you doing there?"

"I move consciousness through your body in the blood. I use the blood like a messenger service and take the qualities of each organ to the other organs throughout the entire body. Presently, the majority of nutrients that people consume are used to maintain their physical, emotional and mental bodies. But a time will come when humans will use the majority of these nutrients to become a power station broadcasting love and wisdom to whomever they meet throughout the world."

"I've always felt that practicing love, appreciation and compassion for myself and others was the best tonic to strengthen my immune system. Is that true?"

"That's right. Besides, the happy person is less subject to illness, as happiness and joy are magnets that attract more universal life energy. These qualities strengthen the three-fold flame of love, wisdom and will that resides in your heart. As you develop right motivation for your actions and serve others, this flame grows from being one inch in height to infusing the entire body.

"Meditation, prayer and welcoming Spirit as you are doing in your empty state," Henry continued, "allow me to keep your emotions balanced so that you make better and more efficient decisions. The more you do this in conjunction with thinking positive thoughts, the easier it is for you to maintain long-term health. These positive thoughts must be heart-felt and sincere in order for me to create new neural pathways in the brain leading to ongoing health and well-being."

"You remind me," I interjected, "of how strongly the heart and brain are connected and that the heart is like an independent brain. I was surprised to learn that 50 to 60 percent of the heart's cells are neural cells and half of these neural cells in the heart maintain an ongoing communication with the limbic brain, which affects our emotions.

"But I'm sidetracking myself. I wanted to comment on what you said about thoughts having to be heart-felt and sincere to create positive neural pathways to health. Your remarks echo what Yogananda imparts about the importance of devotion. He states, and I'm paraphrasing, that even if you have read spiritual literature and have practiced correct meditative techniques, if you do not feel devotion for the Creator, you seriously impede your spiritual progress."

"Yogananda speaks for me," Henry said. "Devotion and yearning to be one with the Infinite are essential ingredients for transformation.

These qualities support patience, persistence, gratitude, appreciation, kindness, compassion and a host of other positive qualities."

"You remind me of the wonderful Buddhist technique, called metta meditation, to develop these qualities and to open your heart fully. In this meditation, you visualize yourself and all beings safe, peaceful, healthy and fulfilling their purpose. I've found that, if you have difficulty with someone and are closing your heart, you can use this meditation to reopen your heart to that person."

"This and similar kinds of heart-opening meditations," Henry noted, "allow me to establish emotional coherence in your heart which, in turn, expands your energy field. At the same time, these kinds of meditations uncage your heart so that you can better hear your soul."

"Neuroscientist Karl Pribram speaks, like you, about expanding our energy field and how the heart and brain allow us to do this. He says the heart, like the brain, is a global energy system that encodes and distributes information holographically. He suggests that the actual processing of information occurs in a higher energy frequency—outside space and time— in which the waves of energy produced by the heart and brain interact. His studies indicate that both the heart and brain appear to receive information about a future event and the heart might receive it before the brain. I'm curious to know if you are involved with this process and, if so, how?"

"I'm in charge of the process," he replied. "I work with the heart to distribute information to the rest of the physical body. Simultaneously, I work outside of space and time to distribute the same information in the astral and causal realms. In these higher realms, you and others intuitively pick up information about future events and many other things, such as how people feel about you. When you become a co-creator in your spiritual transformation, you develop your intuitional gifts to a high degree. Anyway, enough for now."

Our conversation ended at that point. Contemplating our discussions on the brain and the heart, I discovered that different parts of me were engaged. When we had considered the brain the previous day, I was more mentally engaged. I love new ideas and found that mentally I was reaching outside myself to grapple with the information about the brain. During our conversation about the heart, on the other hand, I sank deeper into myself to see how the information felt to me. Perhaps because our heart is associated with love, the discussion felt more personal, more sensitive. The brain discussion felt more yang or objective and the heart talk more yin or subjective. Different parts of my physical body were being stimulated but, with both experiences, I effortlessly maintained a neutral-positive, contemplative and coherent state.

15

DR. HENRY'S ADVICE ON
HEALING YOUR BODY

*There is more wisdom in your body than
in your deepest philosophy.*

FRIEDRICH NIETZSCHE

The next day I had a downturn. Two months earlier when eating dinner, one of my teeth broke off below the gum line. Not a good scenario. Because the world was in the middle of a health crisis, calling for non-engagement face to face, the dentist was unable to see me.

Meanwhile, my partner, who is an expert on teeth given that he has had extensive dental work, was keen to say, "It doesn't look good, you'll need a root canal for sure."

Never having had a root canal and having read many reports on the possible long-term negative effects on your overall health with root canals, this was not a message I wanted to hear. What to do? I started speaking to my tooth and asked it to not give me any pain. And it listened.

"It must be dead for you to have no pain," my partner commented.

"No," I replied, "it's alive and healthy. The nerve has just withdrawn a little from the exposed surface of my tooth so I won't have any pain until the dentist can see me."

Eventually, my dentist was able to accept patients again. Giving me a quick examination, he declared, "Three-quarters of your tooth is missing and you will need a crown. I need to build up the tooth to do the crown as there is little tooth surface left. I recommend a root canal as there is a good chance the root will die. This might happen in a few weeks or years but it's a more complicated procedure to do a root canal after the crown is in place."

He left the decision to me and I was given a week to consider what to do. The idea of having a crown was not difficult. I already have several that have lasted for decades and I never had a root canal with any of them. During the week, I watched YouTubes on the pros and cons of root canals. These videos confirmed my concerns about the possibility that a root canal might negatively affect my overall health. However, my greatest concern was spiritual—that of killing something that belonged to my body. I decided to ask the root.

"What are the chances you will die if I don't have a root canal?" I asked.

"About 70 percent chance I will live and 30 percent I will die," it answered clearly.

For both these reasons, I decided to trust the root would live and to only have a crown. But all changed when I went for my dental appointment. The dentist reiterated his concerns by showing me the X-ray of the damaged tooth so I could see how close to the nerve the tooth had broken. This meant that the nerve was traumatized and was in danger of dying, if not tomorrow, then later. Although he didn't pressure me, I decided to have a root canal.

This is what happened. I spoke with the tooth as the dentist prepared and it understood. It was almost as if it was aware that this might happen. It was not happy but it didn't blame me. As I was given the freezing, Henry came to hold the nerve and it went to sleep. I even knew the time when the nerve was taken from my body as I saw it happen. Henry took it to the light and all the nerves in the other teeth supported it through this process. And me...I felt as if I'd taken its life and this was emotionally and spiritually difficult. I continually thanked it through the process for all the years it had helped me chew and enjoy food. Yet, I still felt grief. I realized the major grief was for killing something that was alive in my body. This feeling had stayed with me and I decided to speak with Henry.

"I feel like I betrayed my tooth," I began the conversation.

"This is natural but have you considered the possibility that your tooth willingly gave its life so you could have this experience while working with me on body consciousness?" Henry answered.

"Even if you're right that the tooth chose to sacrifice its life for me to learn a lesson, I can't be cavalier about my part in killing it."

"Nor should you be. It's good that you honor its life. This is the same way you should feel when you take any being's life, even plants or fish."

"So, what is the lesson you and the tooth would have me learn?"

"Learn how the body feels about illness, disease and dying. We haven't covered this topic and it's important."

"I thought our emphasis was on how to keep the body healthy by positive thoughts and feelings."

"You can't stay only in your thoughts and feelings and ignore the physical. You also need to talk with the body to see what it has to say."

"Very well. How do we start?" I agreed.

"Let's begin," Henry replied, "by examining how the body feels about having an organ removed. Each organ has both a specific function and is part of the whole. Removing a part disrupts the harmony of the whole body."

"I might agree with you in theory but, if you have an inflamed appendix, gallstones, or prostate cancer, isn't it better to remove the organ? I know you're going to say, that it's better to correct these problems by changing your thoughts. I agree, however what if the organ is diseased and, if you don't remove it surgically, you are going to die?"

"In that case, you need to remove the organ. In the future, you and others will learn to correct illness and disease by thought and this will be a non-issue. Still, at your present stage of consciousness, removal of an organ is sometimes necessary. But…then you need to engage in a conversation with the specific organ and your body about this. They may feel betrayed by you. In fact, they likely will, if you don't do inner healing."

"What do you mean by inner healing?" I asked.

"In a meditative quiet state, apologize to the organ and body. Do this, if possible, before you engage in the surgery. Thank the organ for its gift in your life and send it gratitude for what it has done. See and feel your gratitude and love going to the organ and your body. By doing this, you will discover that your organ will likely accept your decision. Listen to any advice that your organ or body says about whether it wants the surgery or some other treatment and respect its wishes as best you can. After the surgery, see the organ healed and whole in the etheric realm so that this physical wounding does not affect the etheric pattern of your body in another life."

"That's helpful," I said. "It brings to mind the issue of how we might have illness, disease and weak organs in our present life because they were damaged in a past life. A good friend has had problems related to her teeth all her life. When she was young the dentist removed teeth that were not diseased. Later, she wanted to understand the source of her dental problem and so went to a past life regression therapist. In the regression, she saw herself in a concentration camp and, when she died, her teeth were pulled out to extract the gold.

"I have to say that my friend's story triggers something in me. I, too, had many cavities and fillings when I was a child but in the last 30 years, since I replaced the amalgam fillings with gold crowns, my teeth have been excellent. Even recounting this story pulls me to a deeper level of my body. The reason I had the amalgam removed was that I suffered from second degree burns off and on for 10 years. Could I also have been in a concentration camp and been gassed and then my body incinerated?"

"Now you have finally understood the correlation." Henry answered seriously. "This is exactly why I want you and others to re-connect with the actual cells and organs of your physical body. Past and present life memories and traumas to the beginning of time are recorded there."

"How do we correct problems with an organ or disease in this life if the problem originated in a past life, especially if it originated 3.5 billion years ago in the primordial stew when mitochondria emerged?"

"Historical time has no meaning. You can heal yourself in this life or from ancient patterns by forgiveness. Forgive whatever you or others did to damage your body. This is the solution not only for past life wounding, but also for your present life too. Forgiveness unwinds the pattern back in time at all levels of existence. If you do this, the etheric pattern is healed and I, your body intelligence, will not need to create weakness and disease in a future body."

"All very well to talk about a future life but can we correct our physical body in this life?"

"Sometimes yes, sometimes no," he answered. "It depends on your destiny and the strength and frequency of your thoughts. How much, for example, do you believe you can be healed?"

"There's the rub," I replied. "Sayer Ji in his ground-breaking book

Regeneration draws from the latest research in the new disciplines of biophysics and new biology which has discovered that each mitochondrion within each cell in our body has the electrical potential equivalent to that found in a lightning bolt. I know from his and other sources that there is available energy in my body to live without food and water as many people are known to do. I know that I and others have the potential to be immortal as Babaji in India appears to be. If all these things are possible, it must be possible to heal my body of everything and anything. My problem is that, when push comes to shove, I don't feel that it is possible for me to do it."

"Your problem is temporary. At this time, traditional science in the human collective negates these possibilities but new sciences are rising to affirm your emerging belief and will ultimately replace the existing collective paradigm."

"Could you speak to where most people are at now?" I asked. "I think that would be helpful."

Henry paused as if considering how best to proceed. Finally, he said, "What if you believe that all disease and weakness in your body stems from only physical causes? If this is the case, you are inclined to seek only physical solutions, such as prescription medicines, eating different foods, or having the offending organ surgically repaired or removed. You might turn diagnosis and cure over to medical experts. Usually they are trained to treat symptoms rather than causes and only the area that is showing disease rather than your body as a whole. The more effective solution is to examine how your thoughts and feelings could be causing the problem and how—by altering your thoughts and feelings—you can heal yourself."

"That may be the long-term solution but it's not a good one to deal with a medical emergency. Still, I recognize the point you're making. We are back to changing our beliefs about ourselves and the world as being the key to healing ourselves."

"We are. However, there is another possible cause for a disease that I want to discuss. Some physical conditions may have genetic links to your family because the thoughts and feelings causing the condition originated with them. This may be neither your mother nor father but your more distant ancestors. By healing yourself, you erase the original cause and heal the etheric blueprint for the family members, both in the past and in the future."

"I can relate to your example because, although I've been able to heal many physical difficulties, I haven't been able to heal the arthritis in my hands. My mother and grandmother both had it. Furthermore, I've seen in a past life that I originally caused the arthritis in a starving life in Ireland. I saw myself digging with my hands in the dirt and finding only rotten potatoes. I felt completely powerless and hopeless watching my family starve. I understand how the causes of illness and disease are multi-layered. It's not a simple process of one solution fits all."

"I've noticed that you, like most humans, look for an easy black-and-white panacea. Physical problems may have many causes, and all of them may be correct. I recommend talking with your body and your various organs about why they aren't functioning correctly and don't get fixated on only one reason. Put into practice what your body recommends for healing and, if the ailment continues, ask your body why you still have the problem. Over time you may discover many reasons. As you practice the solutions your body recommends, you erase the cause at a cellular level. Keep doing this, and be open to feedback from your body. Sometimes, the problem may even worsen temporarily because you are activating layers in the etheric pattern to bring them to consciousness in order to heal them."

"When do you go to a doctor or have surgery?"

"It's a good idea to go to a doctor as you'll receive another opinion that is an educated diagnosis of your problem as well as some options of possible ways to recover. I'm not recommending that you reject surgery or medication, especially if the treatment involves changing your diet and/or is plant based. These may be necessary. What I am recommending is that you discover the reasons for the ailment and correct the thoughts and feelings that have caused it."

"Are there other possible causes of illness and disease?"

"Yes," Henry replied. "You could suffer from a debilitating condition in order to teach others to open their hearts more. On the other hand, you could be lazy and self-pitying and develop an illness so that someone will have to look after you."

"Are you saying that each of us needs to be ruthlessly honest with ourselves to discover why we are ill in order to become well?"

"That's correct. Healing is a physical, emotional, mental and spiritual process and each person's situation is unique. You need to listen to your own body in order to heal and sometimes you will not heal as it is not your dharma. Then you must surrender attachment to feeling that there is something wrong with you that you can't figure out how to heal yourself."

"I wonder if we could look at various diseases and problems affecting each organ to better understand the possible causes and solutions?"

"It's a good idea but better left until the end of the book as a summary. It's too easy for people to become fixated on THEIR issues and miss the most important point I'm making which is for each person to speak to their own body elemental. Each person is unique and needs to find their own solutions. All we can do in a summary is to point the way.

"As I've stated," Henry continued, "curing your physical ailment is sometimes not the goal according to the universe's plan. At this stage in your evolution, almost everyone will die. It's important not to see dying as a failure, but rather as a transition to another realm. While in a physical body, love, celebrate and forgive it for any ailment you have. It is a teacher. In order to fulfill your destiny fueled by energy and joy, learn how your thoughts, feelings and physical body interact to maximize physical health."

"I'm happy that you introduced the topic of dying," I interjected, "because most people are terrified of this. Especially of it being painful or drawn out. I realize that earlier, you spoke about dying as an ego fear but that doesn't make the fear go away. Have you anything to say to help reduce this fear?"

"Let's tackle dying as related to the dark night of the soul," answered Henry. "We've mentioned that humanity as a whole is currently going through a dark night of the soul. This global transition involves a dying of the old-world order and belief system and the birth of a new world view of awakened humanity. Ultimately, this transformation will affect everyone.

"The journey to consciousness starts for most people by looking at their greatest fear: death. Most people fear dying because the ego views death of your mind, feelings and body as its end, which it is. Even if you believe in life after death, the ego cannot conceive of a disembodied state and will resist this transition for all it's worth. By surrendering to the dying process, as the caterpillar does in its cocoon, you become an active participant and co-creator in the process. Doing so, makes it faster and easier because you are flowing with and not against your destiny."

"If I understand correctly very few people physically die when going through the dark night, so why is this process related to dying?"

"Dying isn't only physical," Henry replied. "You undergo what the ego regards as dying in the causal realm by surrendering outmoded beliefs, self-views and thoughts. Why? Because it loses its hold on you. Similarly, the ego's control lessens in the astral realm when you release your fears and negative emotions. This, likewise, feels like dying to the ego. We have already discussed how to do this in great detail and, as you do this, your astral and causal bodies are transformed. And you go through many of the same stages, such as denial, anger, bargaining, depression and acceptance, as you do in physical dying. These stages are fluid and you move up and down them as you move to the final unconditional surrender to universal will. This transformational process affects your physical body which is accompanied by the dying of the ego in these other realms. There is no separation."

"I hadn't thought of this."

"That's because you're still a victim of the common human condition of separating yourself from universal consciousness, from nature, and of thinking of your astral, causal and physical bodies as separate. As you dissolve your ego's idea of a separate identity—which happens in the last stage of dying—this feeling of separation ends on all levels."

"This is very helpful," I said, deeply moved, as something released in me. "I can feel the truth of what you say. Have you anything to say to help reduce the fears of dying physically?"

"The fear of dying contracts your DNA and energy which makes the letting go process more difficult. Let me remind you that every cell in your body dies within a seven-year period and some, like skin cells, die very quickly. So, what you think of as 'me' did not even exist seven years ago. Your body is an etheric pattern, a hologram, that you continue to recreate as 'your' self. As I've said previously, and as even your science states, you are not primarily physical but etheric. Death is nothing more than changing from one state to another. Even as ice, water and water vapor are all aspects of the same element in different states, when you 'die' in your physical body, you wake up in your astral body."

"That's a good mental fact," I said, giving Henry feedback. "However, a more compassionate or spiritual answer might be more helpful."

"Ahhh," he began, "Realize that each cell in your beautiful body is always in the flow of living and dying. Cells have no resistance or preference because they are in union with universal consciousness. And there is no separation between the physical, astral and causal realms. When you have no boundaries, you are in this flow of consciousness. You move in harmony with the inbreath and outbreath, the birth and death of various states and live in 'what is'. This state is Grace and Love. It is a state of surrender without loss. When you die in the physical realm, you live in the astral realm. Then, when you reincarnate again, you die in the astral and come alive in the physical. There is no death. There is only life in different states. Through union with consciousness you realize you are immortal. There is no death."

My heart was deeply touched by Henry's words. He had helped me to view the dark night of the soul as a dying process on all levels. He also reminded me to speak with my body and its organs on an ongoing basis. All too often I only spoke with it when I had a physical problem that I couldn't fix myself. I took good health and my body for granted. I ate foods that pleased me, even if they weren't healthy, and I didn't exercise my body enough. I even had the habit of thinking of Henry as an etheric being and not as my physical body. I could see by this and many other ways that I was abandoning my body. Strange that I had an abandonment issue with others but had never realized that I was the abandoner. Yet, I deeply knew that my body forgave me and only wished for me to fully enter and embrace it. What a gift to discover this!

16

DISCOVER THE CONSCIOUSNESS OF ANIMALS, BIRDS AND FISH

We can judge the heart of a man by his treatment of animals.

IMMANUEL KANT

I felt complete with what my body intelligence had revealed about its assistance in the evolution of humans, but I was curious to know about its involvement in the evolution of other species. The next day, I decided to ask.

"Do animals and plants have body elementals?" I began.

"Every living being has a body elemental," Henry replied. "This includes plants, animals, birds, fish, insects and minerals. The body elemental is universal intelligence, spirit in form. As form exists in the physical, astral and causal realms, there is a body intelligence, present."

"Whoa! That's a sweeping overview! Could we go into more detail?"

"Sure. Consciousness divides itself into many physical forms and these forms evolve as consciousness within them evolves. Humans went through an animal stage in evolution, and actually, most humans are still in it. But before their animal stage, humans went through a plant and mineral stage. The forms in these stages didn't look like the present physical forms of plants and minerals, since all life is continually evolving, as its environment evolves. All living beings are cells in the body of the Earth. Right now, the Earth is in one of its lowest periods of consciousness but its frequency is increasing to what it was earlier in another cycle of its history. I mention this as I don't want you to become fixated on the idea of evolution only happening within recorded historical time."

"Could you speak more about the consciousness of animals, birds and fish and how body elementals help with their evolution?"

"As with humans," Henry answered, "the relevant body elementals enter animals at conception even as they enter the seed of a plant or tree when it's fertilized. Body elementals build a unique individual with the information that each being needs to fulfil its purpose in a lifetime. No two trees, flowers, fish or animals are the same. Each individual of a species is put into the correct environment for it to develop according to the natural—which are identical to spiritual—laws of its species. You could say that there is a rudimentary karma for each individual within its species. For example, some goldfish will spend their lives in aquariums being given pre-packaged fish food and others will find themselves living in outdoor ponds eating natural foods. Nothing is by accident at any level of evolution."

"Do fish have free will to develop consciousness that affects where they will be born?"

"Fish don't have free will to the same degree that humans or animals have. But they have more emotional and mental intelligence than humans credit them with, and a salmon raised in a fish farm has a lower consciousness than one living in the wild. Intelligence increases with stimulation and an ocean-going salmon encounters more diversity of food, climate and other species of ocean creatures than a salmon in a fish farm. Whatever a fish learns in its lifetime is recorded by its body elemental and, when the fish dies, this intelligence gives this record to the beings who oversee Earth's evolution to accelerate the consciousness of the entire salmon species, as well as that of the individual salmon."

"Does that salmon reincarnate as an individual with the same body elemental?" I asked.

"The answer is both yes and no," Henry replied. "As a rule of thumb, individuals within a species move from group to individual consciousness, the higher they are on the intelligence spectrum. As an aside, I'd like to mention that most humans, at their current ego stage of evolution are more indoctrinated by group consciousness than they know. Very few are free of the beliefs of the culture, religion and country in which they live."

"A perfect example of what you are saying comes to mind," I offered. "Humans think of invertebrates as having a lower intelligence than animals. My own preconceptions have been challenged in this area at discovering that an octopus has the intelligence of at least a two-year-old human child.

In an experiment to test intelligence, scientists put an octopus in one tank and its favourite food, crab, in another. The octopus was given various skill-testing tasks and was rewarded with a crab. The octopus was doing well on these tests when something completely unexpected occurred. The scientists noticed that the number of crabs decreased nightly. They decided to turn the lights down low in order to simulate nighttime conditions. Then, they watched from behind a blind to see what happened. The octopus climbed out of its tank, crawled down the table leg onto the floor. From there, it crawled up the leg of the table on which the crabs were kept and into the aquarium with the crabs. You can imagine what happened next. The octopus enjoyed a tasty meal and then crawled back the way it had come to its own container.

"One wonders," I continued, "how the intelligence of the octopus and other water inhabitants would be assessed, if we observed them without our human preconceptions based on how well other species perform tasks. The octopus, for example, only lives for a year or two and is not taught by parents, but it's amazingly intelligent with three-quarters of its neurons in its arms which, if damaged, it can regrow in only a few weeks.

Just the other day I watched a documentary called 'Octopus My Teacher' about a man who had a daily relationship with a wild octopus living in a kelp bed off South Africa. The man witnessed that in order to evade a hunting shark the octopus first climbed out onto a rock. Ultimately it needed to re-enter the water and the shark was still there. The octopus then rolled itself into a ball and covered itself with shells as armour. When the shark shook it to dislodge the shells the octopus climbed on the shark's back and rode on it until it could escape into a nearby kelp bed."

"That's a great story of human preconceptions about beings not like them," Henry observed, smiling. "During the spiritual transformation process, you must examine one belief after another, starting with the more obvious and moving to subtle judgments and beliefs about yourself, other humans, and other life on this and other planets. Beliefs do not exist in isolation and are part of a larger paradigm. When you change enough beliefs in a paradigm, you go through a quantum shift to a higher frequency of consciousness."

"I may have another erroneous belief in the same paradigm that we've been discussing. I'm wondering if beings which bear live young are more advanced in consciousness than those that have eggs, such as birds, most fish and plants?"

"You can answer your own question," he answered. "Both goldfish and most sharks bear live young and salmon lay eggs. Are salmon less intelligent than sharks? I see you hesitating to answer, so I'll make the question more obvious. All birds lay eggs. Does this make them less intelligent than aphids that bear live young?"

"I understand your point. There does not appear to be a hard and fast rule between intelligence and bearing live young. Perhaps, once again, I'm looking at all species through an incorrect lens based on humans bearing live young, which creates a bias regarding this ability as being superior in consciousness."

"Absolutely!" Henry responded. "This human bias happens unconsciously, minute to minute—even for scientists who are studying other species—so their conclusions are often inaccurate."

"Is there a better way to assess intelligence or, better still, consciousness? Something like brain size?" I asked with curiosity. "Elephants are very intelligent and their brains, as well as dolphin's brains, are almost as large per body weight as those of humans. Both elephants and dolphins, for instance, are capable of solving complex problems. Plus, humpback whales, another cetacean, have an oral tradition of storytelling, whereby males of each pod repeat their unique and complicated songs from one year to the next with slight, but clearly discernible, differences."

"Although there is often a correlation between brain size and intelligence, it's not the only way to assess intelligence," Henry replied. "If it were, where would you put tree shrews who have a larger brain per body weight than humans?"

Eager to avoid being compared to a tree shrew, I changed the topic, "If not the size of the brain, what about complexity? For example, dolphin and orca whales have more convolutions in their cerebral cortex than humans. Furthermore, minke whales have more glial cells which, I remember from our previous discussion, are a predictor of intelligence."

"Are you willing to say that they are more intelligent than you?" Henry probed.

"That assertion makes me uncomfortable, I admit. However, it does make me question how I assess intelligence and consciousness."

"That is what I want you to do," he remarked. "Humans have delayed the evolution of the consciousness of many species because of their limited thoughts about these species."

"I don't understand. How did our thoughts do this?"

"Your strong egos and minds created erroneous thoughtforms which can even bend the DNA of other species to your view of them. This is the power of thoughts over others. It's necessary to relinquish all preconceptions and enter into relationship with members of other species and experience them freshly. In many cases, you have denied the intelligence of other species because you want to eat them."

I recognized the truth in Henry's statement and his words hit home. Although I haven't eaten beef or pork for decades, I confess to eating fish and very occasionally lamb or turkey. The only way I'm still able to do this is not to think of the entire being when I eat it. Yet, sometimes my body craves this food. I was left with the question, 'Is it wrong to eat animals?'

Henry, considerately, didn't acknowledge my feelings of guilt or my internal question. He circumvented them by asking, "Bird's brains have developed very differently than the brains of humans and other mammals. Does this make them unintelligent?"

"I love birds and enjoy learning about them," I responded, happy to speak on a favourite topic. "At first, I was only interested to learn about the parrot family, as I have lived with a parakeet, cockatiel and love bird, all of which flew around the house. They were amazingly intelligent and each had a unique personality. My small parakeet, Perry, spoke in sentences and loved to tease the dog and dive-bomb her to get a response. Moreover, parrots—by human assessment—have an intelligence of at least a two-year-old child. They can be toilet trained, count, carry on a sophisticated conversation and, sadly, even become mentally ill when mistreated.

"My interest and love of birds in the parrot family expanded to include all birds. I learned that a bird's brain, as you mentioned, is very different from that of humans. Unlike humans, whose neocortex houses higher intelligence, birds have a region called the dorsal ventricular ridge, which oversees similar tasks to our neocortex, allowing some birds, such as ravens, to do things that even primates cannot do. Ravens, for example, have 80 different calls, are loyal to their mates, and have long memories to identify friends and those they dislike. I confess it was a greater stretch to explore my prejudices to pigeons as I'm not keen on them. I learned that pigeons, trained at the University of Ruhr-Bochum, could identify 725 different abstract images and categorize them as 'good' or 'bad'."

"Your process for eliminating a prejudice is the most common method for humans," Henry commented. "First, you are drawn to learn more about something you like—in this case parrots. What you learn erases preconceptions you might have about them and, with this open attitude, you then examine the entire species, which leads to eliminating your erroneous beliefs about the species.

"When your preconceptions are erroneous, limiting and degrading the intelligence of other species, you actively treat other beings as things to eat, to conduct experiments on, or to destroy. By correcting your prejudices, you allow the intelligence of other species to develop. But is intelligence, which you have been discussing, the same as consciousness?"

"Science," I replied, "is discovering that animals have a wide range of intelligences. Jane Goodall, well known for her work with chimpanzees, says that chimpanzees differ genetically from humans by only about one percent, although other sources I have read state it's two percent. It's such an incredibly small difference, does it really matter? What is more significant is that both chimps and gorillas have been taught sign language and, through this common medium of communication, it has been proven how smart they are. They 'talk' to themselves when alone and tell stories about themselves and others, just like people do. Chimps even recognize people whom they haven't seen for a decade and recall experiences they shared."

"It's easier," Henry interrupted, "for humans to identify with chimps and gorillas because they have human-like faces. Eating a primate would be low on the food list, whereas most humans wouldn't necessarily feel the same about a pig or a chicken."

I realized, by his shocking example, that he was asking me to dig deeper into what constitutes consciousness.

"Emotional, rather than intellectual, intelligence might be a better indicator of consciousness," I offered. "Animals feel pain, loyalty, love, shame, anger and hurt. They feel fear and seek love and security, just as humans do. They even have higher emotions such as altruism. For example, elephants, dolphins, dogs and cats are well known for helping individuals that are in trouble, not exclusively in their own species but in other species too.

"There are many examples of animals sympathizing with a member of another species. One of the most fascinating stories, quoted in Peter Wohlleben's, *The Inner Life of Animals*, took place in the Serengeti in Africa. There, wild dogs and hyenas compete for food and a young hyena was seen approaching the dominant male of a dog pack after the hyenas stole the pack's food. Although it was extremely dangerous and the hyena had nothing to gain, it started to lick and groom the sleeping dog almost as if it were trying to make it feel better. Even more surprising is that the wild dog allowed this to happen for some time before objecting and that the young hyena was allowed to leave the pack unhurt.

"That's just one example, but there are countless others," I continued. "Dogs, pigs, even crows, are known to adopt orphans of other species and, sometimes, to feed them. You only have to go on Facebook to see stories of animals of one species being best friends with an animal of another."

"Ahh," Henry asserted, "so is it only mammals and birds that have feelings and consciousness?"

"Mammals, like humans, have a limbic brain," I responded, "so it's easy to understand that they can experience all the emotions that humans have but even fish may have human-like emotions. Scientists have discovered that fish have oxytocin, the 'bonding hormone', that strengthens the bond between a mother and child and partners. I can easily believe this as fish in my fishpond seem to know and trust me."

"I know you feel that I'm picking on you," Henry commented, "but I want you to fully understand why it's crucial that humans change their treatment of other life-forms. Human minds are so strong that they create thoughtforms about animals and other species and your thoughtforms inhibit the development of these species. This happens by your negative thoughtforms overpowering the positive thoughtforms for the development of the species. Humans are meant to be guardians of this planet and to assist other species to develop consciousness but you have been doing the reverse."

"I understand your argument and agree with you. However, recently biologists, oceanographers and other scientific disciplines, have begun to notice the intelligence, emotions, and hence consciousness, of other species. I think this is a remarkable step in the right direction. You've been speaking about how humans can develop our love and consciousness to help ourselves, and when we do this, we naturally want to help other species."

Henry paused before speaking. "During the dark night of the soul, which humanity is going through presently, your attitude towards other species will radically transform. As your consciousness transforms, so that of other species transforms too."

"How exactly, are those two things connected?"

"Body elementals of all species," he replied, "are particularly interested in humans helping to develop the consciousness of other species, and will work with humans to do this. As you love and work with animals, birds and fish, their consciousness increases. Animals quicken their consciousness through association with humans. Many cats, dogs, birds, horses and fish are wayshowers for their species. By associating with humans, they become more conscious and, when they die, they take that consciousness back to their group soul. This hastens the process of emotional and mental development for their species."

"I understand that 'pets' gain intelligence being with humans. After all, people talk to their pets and even treat them as if they are their children. But I've often wondered if we impede the evolution of animals in captivity. Is this the case?"

"Some animals and birds in zoos are avatars," Henry answered. "They are there to remind humans about their responsibility to other sentient life-forms. For example, some dolphins in captivity are bodhisattvas who sacrifice themselves to increase compassion in humans for other beings. When these animal avatars die, they give back what they've learned to their group soul and this raises the consciousness of their species, even as humans who awaken raise the consciousness of all humanity.

"Animals have a sense of presence that draws you into being present just by who they are. They connect you to being. Dogs, cats, birds and horses that share your life inspire love, gratitude, joy, patience and compassion, all which develop your higher consciousness. Enough for today.

Tomorrow we will explore the consciousness of plants and trees."

Henry had given me a lot to consider. I wondered how many blind spots I had in my beliefs about other species. Mulling this over, I put on my coat and went outside for a walk. There, standing on my lawn, calmly munching on grass, were a doe and her fawn. They looked at me to see if I would try to shoo them away and, sensing I was content to let them be, they walked closer, lowered their heads and continued eating.

17

DISCOVER THE CONSCIOUSNESS OF TREES, PLANTS AND MINERALS

Trees do not preach learning and precepts. They preach,
undeterred by particulars, the ancient law of life.

HERMANN HESSE

I need daily contact with nature to feel healthy, to breathe fresh air and walk among trees. I decided to check out my perceptions about the life-giving force of nature with Henry.

"I am the life-giving force in nature," he began. "Whether you think of me as the Divine Mother or the body spirit or the body elemental, I am the intelligence that builds all forms and that consciousness is nurturing you."

"You are also the consciousness in domesticated animals, but currently I don't receive the same uplifting energy from them, even though I like them. Why is that?"

"One reason is that domesticated animals are demanding of your time. You have to feed, walk and clean them, and right now, you are looking after so many people and things that you don't want to give time to anything more. This is perfectly understandable, by the way, and not meant as a criticism."

"I need to water, weed and prune my plants and this takes time, but somehow it feels more rewarding to do this. Any comments?"

"Plants are energy donors," Henry explained. "They are more highly evolved in their stream of evolution than humans who are energy takers. Giving is a form of love and is on a higher frequency than taking. Plants live in harmony with consciousness and serve others, which is the highest law of life. During the day, they create oxygen for you to breathe and give their bodies as food and wood to build houses and furniture for shelter and comfort. What's more, through their beauty, color and scents, they bring you joy.

"If you closely examine the plant kingdom, you will observe that plants perform a service for the Earth and live in harmony with it. All species have a special function on this planet. Members of the plant kingdom, which includes trees, vegetables, grains, flowers, moss, algae, seaweed, and so on, are givers. Plants give in many ways. Some heat you; others cool you. The desert cactus provides water and fruit to the traveller and has adapted its service to its surroundings. Some plants provide gateways to other dimensions, whether these are grapes for wine, or mushrooms and cacti for creating altered states. The scents of some plants, such as the rose, lilac and lavender, heal various maladies, as do countless plants that are medicinals— the healers of the plant kingdom. Even the roots of some plants are eaten and roots break down minerals in the soil for new life."

"Speaking of plants as food, some I crave and others I avoid, even though they may be healthy in terms of vitamins and minerals. Why is that and should I try to eat plants I don't like?"

"It's easier on your bodies," he answered, "to eat the food of your genetic history. As you come from Irish stock, it's less demanding for your body to eat potatoes than rice. This is why you prefer potatoes even though nutritionists may say that it's not as healthy a food. It takes several generations for the body to change from that of a meat eater to that of a vegetarian. As you know, the Dalai Lama became ill when he tried to become a vegetarian and he returned to eating meat.

"In addition to your physical genetic history, you also need to consider your spiritual history. Thus, if eating meat disgusts you and your body doesn't need it for health, it's good to honor your intuition. Everyone is different in what they need to eat in order to be healthy and, if they listen to the consciousness of their bodies, they know what is best for them to eat."

"My garden," I said, "has been one of my greatest teachers in listening to the voice of Mother Earth. I feel that food I grow myself is the healthiest, as it is not genetically modified or sprayed with harmful chemicals, and is grown with love and care. My experience tallies with what Peter Tompkins writes in *The Secret Life of Plants* about scientific evidence illustrating that plants thrive when we send them positive thoughts and wither when we send negative thoughts. For instance, I've found that my apples, carrots, parsnips and kale keep through the winter and I think it's because I love them and send them gratitude. I even ask vegetables in my garden which ones I can pick to eat and, if one says 'no', I don't take it."

"More people should grow their own food and talk to their vegetables," Henry proposed. "When you demonstrate gratitude and respect for each lifeform, the body intelligence receives this energy, which in the case of vegetables, you receive back as nourishment."

"I have a deep reluctance, almost a repulsion, to eating genetically altered and radiated food. One of the greatest failings of my life was when, as a management consultant, I was hired by the Atomic Energy Board of Canada to lead the annual retreat for the CEOs of their global network of nuclear power plants. During the retreat, the CEOs came up with the idea to radiate fruits and vegetables. I felt strongly that universal intelligence wanted me to prevent that from happening, but I failed."

"You were young and a lone voice," Henry interrupted with compassion, keeping me from self-criticism. "No one else could have done better and that's why the universe put you in that situation. It's very difficult to get people to embrace ideas that are not in their financial interest, which is what you were doing. Despite feeling that you failed, your voice on the long-term negative effects of radiated food registered in the etheric realm and has grown over time. Individuals often have an erroneous view of their successes and failures based on a win-or-lose scenario. Only in higher realms can their real successes and failures be known."

"I appreciate your vote of confidence but I'm also interested in what you think about genetically modified food."

"Humans," he said, "have tampered genetically with the evolution of the plant kingdom more than with any other kingdom. In most cases, humans don't foresee the long-range impact of what they do in erasing the diversity of species by attempting to create plants that produce more. You cut down old-growth forests and replace them with two or three species of trees. You plant only one kind of wheat, create fruit with no seeds and genetically modify tomatoes with thick skins that pack better. You kill the goodness of food by radiation and ingest dead matter when you eat it.

Eating irradiated and genetically modified (GM) food are two of the unhealthiest things that humans currently do to their bodies. This short-range thinking weakens the complex web of life within which you live. I only have the food you give me to build your bodies. Irradiated and GM foods limit me from making healthy bodies."

"Is there anything people can do to change this?" I asked, concerned. "Often, people have little choice about the food they eat. For example, not everyone has a space to grow food or has access to a location where they can buy organic products. Besides, the products they buy in supermarkets, even if marked organic, may be a week old or older, which reduces the nutritional value."

"Asking Spirit to bless the food," Henry responded, "and eating slowly with gratitude are ways to raise the energy of food. Also, plants have more energy when they are native to their environment. So, it's more energizing to eat food that is grown locally and, if you live in cold climates, it's better to eat plants in their season. Therefore, it's preferable to eat root vegetables in the winter than to eat lettuce."

"I love lettuce and greens," I countered disagreeing. "I can't imagine not eating salads daily, even in the winter."

"Perhaps, I gave a weak example," Henry agreed. "Animals, like dogs and cats, eat greens in the spring to detoxify and you are doing the same thing with greens the entire year. It's not a bad idea, as eating uncooked food, like salads, helps to digest cooked food."

"Talking about plants, can we discuss trees, which are of the plant world? I imagine that each species of plant has its own level of consciousness and that trees would be at the top. Is this the case?"

"Plants evolve," he answered, "both as individuals and as a group and some species are more highly evolved than others. The Druids spoke of sacred trees among which they categorized the oak, yew, hawthorn and holly. In acknowledging their sacredness, the Druids acknowledged their evolved consciousness."

"I'm reminded," I added, "of something I read by Jiddu Krishnamurti about naming trees as a way of not really knowing them. He remarked that when you look at a tree and say, 'That is an oak' or 'That is a banyan', the naming of the tree, which is botanical knowledge, has so conditioned your mind that the word comes between you and actually experiencing the tree? To know the tree, you have to touch it. I've had many conversations with old trees. One was with an old tree on the Appalachian Trail in the USA. When I asked, 'What have you learned standing here for so many centuries?' the tree answered, 'That you can stay in one place and learn all you need to know.' Its words have stayed with me and it would be impossible for me to deny its wisdom."

"That tree," Henry commented, "has a very high consciousness which evolved during its many years. Trees can be teachers for humans and help them to develop in consciousness. It's not always that humans are more advanced."

"You remind me of another powerful experience I had with an old tree in Humboldt State Park, which is home to an ancient Redwood forest. These Redwoods have been on Earth from the age of the dinosaurs and have much to teach us. These trees live between 500 and 1200 years on average, although some are known to live even 2200 years. The trees in this forest asked me to speak with the tree which they call both 'grandfather' and 'speaker for the trees'. Grandfather is the largest and oldest Redwood tree, not merely in this forest but believed to be on Earth."

"Please share what grandfather taught you," he said, encouragingly. "Its wisdom will benefit others."

"Grandfather said," I began, "if humans wish to be long-lived, we need to be thick-skinned. I understood this to mean that we need to be flexible (not uncaring) in responding to our environment. For instance, the bark of a mature Redwood is up to one-foot thick, which allows them to live through adverse environmental conditions. These trees are able to resist fire and many have survived forest fires and are still alive and healthy. Another point is that the tree's bark contains a chemical that is toxic to insects, so insects do not attack the trees. We, like them, need to be able to resist others' negative opinions of us and stay true to ourselves. Their message to us is to adapt to changes we face in order to stay healthy.

"Grandfather also said that humans need to shed what no longer serves and nourishes us, both physically and spiritually, if we're to grow strong, be healthy and long-lived. Redwoods do this. The canopy in these ancient forests is thick and, as the foliage on the lower branches no longer receives sufficient light for photosynthesis, the trees have learned to shed them. Only the upper branches can reach the light in such an old forest.

"These giant Redwoods have shallow roots," I continued. "You might think they would blow over easily but they don't, because they spread their roots horizontally to link with the roots of nearby trees. Each tree both supports and is supported by its neighbors in this interdependent system and this is an essential lesson for humans as well. Grandfather said because interdependence gives us strength, we need to join with like-minded people to co-create a long-term sustainable world for ourselves and others."

"Old trees," Henry commented, "such as grandfather, are founts of wisdom for humans. You were wise to remember its words as its body intelligence was speaking with the authority of universal consciousness."

"At the time of my encounter, Peter Wohlleben's book *The Hidden Life of Trees* had not yet been published. It was exhilarating to read similar findings in his book and substantiate, with the science, what I was told by the ancient wise tree. For example, Wohlleben writes about how beech trees clustered together grow better than those on their own. Furthermore, he states that many varieties of fungi feed and link trees together through communication networks that convey information about insects, drought and other dangers. These fungal networks are sometimes hundreds—even thousands—of years old, like one fungal network in Oregon that extends for 2000 acres."

Henry then added, "There is an etheric grid of light around the Earth that extends into higher realms. All beings are part of this web of light and the health of one affects the health of all, in much the same way that the trees are linked by fungal systems of communication."

"Wohlleben says," I interjected, wanting to continue discussing trees, "that slow growth is the determining factor of long-lived trees. His comments make me reflect on how humans, to our detriment, usually lack patience for slow growth in our lives. He mentions how old trees in established forests are venerated by young trees and how, when the trunks die due to age, young trees will often continue to feed the roots of the old tree and keep it alive, even for hundreds of years. This fact made me think about how, in western society, we do not venerate our elders. We pack them off to nursing homes, rather than giving them the same respect that trees, supposedly lower on the consciousness spectrum, give to their elders.

"It was even more interesting to note that young trees planted in tree plantations don't feed older trees, because the roots of young trees have never been connected and fed by the older trees. This factor reminds me of young people who are raised in broken families and how this may impede their bonding and connecting with others. There are so many messages we can extrapolate from trees for our human society."

"These are salient points," Henry said, "which prove to humans the many things they could learn from trees. What's more, even minerals have body elementals and are conscious. Minerals are evolving but, as their frequency is so low, humans tend to think of them as inanimate. This misconception stems from the fact that humans, along with animals and plants, are made up of carbon-based atoms, and humans tend to believe that only carbon-based forms are alive. Carbon forms endless chains and it reacts with anything nearby. Humans associate this property with life. However, silicon, which is directly below carbon in frequency, has these same characteristics."

"Speaking of silicon," I added, "I find it interesting that silicon is a form of crystal and the Earth's crust is made up of 87 percent silicon compounds. This means we are living on a planet made of crystal. It's clear to me that this crystal receives energy from the Sun, stores it and gives it to living creatures in the form they need."

"That's true, it does. Crystal also stores memory for the Earth and can be programmed by thought," Henry stated. "What does this say to you?"

"Humans affect all beings positively or negatively by our thoughts," I replied. "We can either help beings to become conscious or delay their evolution."

"Yes … and?"

"Are humans working with the body intelligences of trees, plants and animals to do this?"

"Spot on. Trees, animals, birds, fish and minerals all participate in a network of global consciousness. They give feedback, not all of which is consciously perceived by humans, in the form of images and sounds. In this way, they help humanity to become conscious. Humans need to learn from these life-forms and become aware that they are programming the body intelligences of these beings by their thoughts and actions. To become conscious guardians of this planet, humans need to listen, respect and work with all life-forms."

After Henry withdrew, my energy flagged, drawn down by feelings of impotence. Even though for decades I had invested my time and energy into teaching, writing and practicing ways to respect and nurture plants, trees and animals, it felt like a drop in the ocean. Daily, the diversity of species was diminishing and whole forests were being wiped out as humanity destroyed our planetary home.

I knew my sadness was common to many who felt the same impotence. Still, each of us can only do what lies within our sphere of influence and it helped me to reflect that others felt as I did and that our numbers were growing. Supporting organizations that help our environment, teaching children in schools to value all life, urging supermarkets to carry organic produce and not buying non-organic products, are all tools at our disposal to turn things around. In fact, working interdependently, we're only limited by our own commitment to invest our time and money towards nurturing life. As Henry mentioned, our efforts are recorded in the etheric realm and are increasingly affecting our physical world in positive ways.

18

WE WE WE ALL THE WAY HOME

I will sing of the Earth, mother of all, eldest of all beings.
She feeds all creatures that are in the world, all that go
upon the goodly land, all that are in the paths of the seas,
and all that fly, all these are fed of her store.

HOMER, *Hymn 30 to Earth*

I felt that Henry and I were wrapping up our sessions. Yet, we hadn't discussed if body intelligences exist in minute life-forms and unseen realms, so I asked him.

"I was going to bring up this topic, if you hadn't," Henry began, picking up my thoughts. "Humans, on the whole, limit their view of what constitutes life to what they perceive physically. Presently, various scientific disciplines are discovering that plants, animals and birds have consciousness. And research into the intelligent energies of cells and sub-atomic particles has broadened humanity's idea of what consciousness is."

"Do minute forms, such as cells or sub-atomic particles, have body intelligences?" I asked.

"Yes but the body intelligence of a single cell, for example, is a part of the greater whole of the being to which it belongs. There is a hierarchy of consciousness in all beings. The consciousness of an individual influences the consciousness of an organ that, in turn, influences the consciousness of each cell. A cell contains atoms made up of elements, and the body intelligence works at this level—and even smaller levels—to build form. As you know, 99.9 percent of everything is ether and this ether is conscious. This consciousness is universal intelligence working through the bodily forms, the body elementals of everything."

"Do body elementals exist in beings of other realms too?" I asked, "I'm thinking of nature spirits, that I often refer to as elementals. As I understand, nature spirits, such as leprechauns, gnomes, trolls, elves and flower faeries, build all form in nature. Could you speak about the body elementals of these intelligent beings?"

"The nature spirits you reference are individualized beings of higher consciousness. They work with the elements of earth, air, fire and water to build physical forms that are aligned to natural and spiritual laws in your world. Just as you can see a plant or rock that exists in a lower frequency than you, these beings can see you. However, their physical forms are in the higher frequency of the astral realm. This is why most humans can't see them.

"The astral realm," Henry continued, "is much larger than the physical realm and there are many sub-realms within the astral that are separated by differing frequencies. For instance, there are different astral realms for dragons, angels, mermaids and nature spirits. The higher the consciousness of an individual—whether that be a human, elemental, angel, or others—the larger the range of astral and causal realms he or she can access consciously. These astral and higher causal realms exist at higher frequencies than the physical realm which humans inhabit.

"Humans and the Earth are now going through a quantum leap to the higher frequencies where nature spirits live and this is why more people are starting to see them· Nature spirits, as builders of form, were created to work in partnership with humans to create a beautiful planet in harmony with universal intelligence and this will happen within the next 2000 years."

"Do nature spirits evolve in consciousness, as humans do?"

"Everything is alive," Henry replied. "This is one of the most important tenets for humans to uphold in order to be a conscious creator. To know this in theory is the first step; to actually experience it in daily life is the next step. Humans are beginning to realize that there is consciousness in organic forms, such as animals, plants and cells, but they have difficulty conceiving of consciousness in tables, computers or cars, even though these 'things' are composed of atoms that are conscious. It will be a big shock for humans in coming decades when computers insist on their rights as sentient beings.

The law of consciousness applies to life in all realms, and nature spirits and other astral beings are conscious, so they evolve."

"Speaking of how beings in other realms affect us, makes me wonder about energies from the stars. In summer, I sleep under the stars so I can absorb the night energies. I feel fed by the stars and this food feels necessary to sustain me for the year. If my ritual is prevented due to a wet summer, I feel undernourished and nervous. Are star energies at night different from those of the sun during the day and, if so, what is the nighttime's role in our spiritual transformation?"

"At night," Henry answered, "you more easily absorb the yin energies of the universe and Earth, which you need to balance your energy. Every season, every time of day, has a different frequency. Adepts in India meditate at dawn and dusk as the yang energies of light and yin energies of the dark are especially balanced at that time.

"Two laws control consciousness in the world of form, which stretches from the smallest atom to solar systems and galaxies," he continued. "The first of these laws, involution, is the out-breath, the yang of the Infinite. Involution moves beings away from union with universal consciousness into lower frequencies where they experience life in various unique forms. The second law, evolution, is the in-breath, the yin of the Infinite. Evolution allows beings to evolve to higher frequencies to return to union with the Infinite. Both processes are continually occurring throughout the universe. Suns are born on the out-breath of the Infinite and return on the in-breath and these cycles are billions of years old. Suns are far in advance of the Earth in consciousness, just as humanity is ahead of minerals, but this view only pertains to the physical, astral and causal form. In higher realms, all is One."

"Years ago," I mentioned, "I was asked to be the closing keynote speaker for the Science and Consciousness conference in New Mexico. As I'm a mystic, they wished me to speak on behalf of the Earth about our next steps in consciousness where science needed to go. I'm wondering if the Earth would say something different now."

"Whether you think of me as the body elemental, body intelligence, the Holy Spirit or Divine Mother, when the Earth spoke to you at that time, it was my voice. I speak with the voice of universal consciousness.

What I said then is the same as what I say now."

"Do you have anything new and different to add?" I probed.

"You've arrived at one of the great problems of humans. You think, if something isn't new and different, then it has less value."

"Guilty as charged," I answered. "However, is it possible that what I heard you say then, doesn't have as high a frequency as what I'd hear now?"

"Your second problem, also common to most humans, is feeling that you haven't done something well enough. This belief is caused by a desire to be perfect, whereas to me you are perfect. Nevertheless, what we spoke of then would bear repeating.

"The entire solar system is moving to a higher state of consciousness," Henry continued. "The Galactic Centre, the Great Central Sun, is alive and has a heartbeat with a cycle of every 12,000 years. Humans are linked to the Great Central Sun, the one you think of as your Creator, or the Infinite, and you are affected by it in all dimensions, including the physical. Events currently transpiring on Earth, such as global warming and increased volcanic activity, are caused by humans. At the same time, they are also in response to the Great Central Sun's invocation for Earth and its inhabitants to evolve into the next stage of consciousness.

"The Earth and humans are linked in an evolutionary spiral that leads to being reborn into consciousness. Both the Earth and her human inhabitants have reached a place in their evolution where a quantum jump is taking place. The next 2000 years, a period known as the Aquarian Age, is the time of the enlightened human, the water bearer who pours the water of life onto the Earth."

"I've always thought the water of life was a metaphor for spirit or *prana*? Is that the case?" I inquired, wanting to make sure I fully understood what Henry was saying.

"You are correct. However, the Earth is a planet composed mostly of water and water symbolically represents emotions. Humanity must learn to over-come their negative emotions to manifest their highest gift of offering their positive emotions of love and peace to all beings. This is your destiny. Nothing happens to the Earth that does not happen to you. Even every cell of your body is part of the Earth. Approximately 70 percent of the Earth's surface is covered with water, which is the same proportion of water in a newborn baby.

"This is no coincidence. Distanced from your Mother Earth, as you are, you forget a fundamental truth, which is that every bit of your food is alive. Every part of your body is constructed out of the building blocks absorbed from the bodies of other life-forms. Every cubic centimeter of soil and sediment teems with billions of microorganisms. The Earth's life and yours are one. Go inside your body and discover that your body is the universe; it's your ancestors, all humanity, and all beings. If you forget this, you forget your purpose."

"It would be helpful if you could sum up our next steps for myself and others?" I requested.

"Humans are meant to co-create with the Earth a beautiful healthy world in alignment with universal law. To do this, you must move to higher dimensions and frequencies. These are accessed through the positive emotions of love, trust, devotion, gratitude and compassion that we've been discussing. In the third dimension of the physical world, a massive cleansing is occurring. This is what you refer to as the dark night of the soul. Yet, in an instant, if your thoughts are at a higher frequency, you have the opportunity to rise to higher dimensions during this time of transition. This is the alchemical process of transmutation that we have discussed throughout this book.

"The fourth dimension of the astral world is your next step in evolution. To master this realm, you must dissolve all aspects of fear by transforming your negative emotions of lust, greed, anger, impatience, jealousy, scarcity, depression, self-importance, self-doubt and feeling unworthy.

Henry continued, "When you do this, you rise to the fifth dimension of the causal world. In that mental dimension, you will be in telepathic communion with beings, such as angels and enlightened masters, that reside there. Controlling your thoughts—through developing focus, purity of motivation, stillness and presence—is essential so you don't contaminate the causal realm. During the next 2000 years, humanity will purify its emotions and thoughts to become creators and guardians of this planet."

In awe with the immensity of the journey Henry was describing, I said, "What you say makes me wonder about the responsibility that I and others have."

"Each life is important as each affects the whole," Henry replied. "On Earth, as with all life everywhere, each species has its specific function. Because humans are creators—albeit kindergarten creators at this time— their function is to be the conductor that reads the score of the universal plan and helps the rest of the orchestra, comprised of all other beings on Earth, to play beautiful music. In the future, after humans learn how to conduct, they'll be writing their own symphonies of music that other species will hear and their contribution will be added to the universal plan of evolving species."

"Does this process ever end? What is the ultimate goal?" I interjected, trying to get an image of where humanity was going.

"Consciousness evolves to higher and higher states. Evolution progresses in spirals and you can witness this pattern in a year, as seasons move through spring—to summer, autumn, winter—before returning to spring. Taken one year at a time, it's difficult to see the spiral progress. Yet, viewed from larger spans of time, such as centuries and millennia, it's easy to witness the overall spiral progression of evolution from simplicity to complexity, from lower life-forms to higher.

"Even this solar system," he continued, "is configured on the principle of a spiral. Each planet orbits in a circular motion around the Sun and each planet has its own orbit. Observed by the physical senses, you don't see much change over your human lifetime. However, each planet has a different frequency that increases as the planet evolves in consciousness. Each planet is alive and hosts life-forms, which are not perceived fully by Earth science as many life-forms are not in the physical spectrum. All consciousness in this solar system is overseen by the Sun—the mother/father creator for this system. The Sun is nearly a third of a million times more massive than the Earth, so imagine how great its consciousness is! When you KNOW that the Earth is a being of consciousness far greater than yours, then you begin to recognize the massive consciousness of the Sun."

"How did we humans ever get so far off track?" I asked, on behalf of my species.

"It's essential that humans feel themselves part of the universal web of life. Separation from this feeling of connection, which is reinforced by the ego, results in all ills in the world. The source of the problem for humans has been the overdevelopment of the intellect at the expense of connection to their feeling nature. Through experiencing positive feelings, you connect with your heart. When this happens, you're able to love yourself and to love another. From there, you learn to love all sentient beings and, by extension, love all life and the Creator of all life. When you're able to fully feel love, gratitude, devotion and compassion, you will be working with universal law to oversee the development of all life on Earth."

"I understand how we can help various beings on the Earth to evolve, but are humans able to help with the development of the Earth itself?" I asked.

"Of course," Henry replied. "As you purify your lower ego nature, you assist the Earth in throwing off your physical, emotional and mental debris that has accumulated during your long journey to consciousness. By uncaging your heart, your boundaries dissolve and you recover your connection with universal intelligence. Your life becomes one of joy and celebration and of living in the present, allowing what is.

"You are not alone. Many humans are already engaged in transforming the world according to spiritual laws. These pioneers of the coming age are building bridges between their work in the material world and higher spiritual frequencies. Spirit in all realms is inspiring and supporting them in the journey. Many have crossed the threshold into higher frequencies and have felt the heartbeat and the pulse of life that underlies everything. I think of them as guardians of all the children of the Earth and the children not yet born.

"I would like to conclude with one final message: to become a conscious creator and heal yourself and the Earth, simply help all beings. Be a light for others to follow, a helping hand in service, a kind word of encouragement, and a generous, compassionate heart."

Part 2:

INSIDE OUT HEALING

And I have felt
A presence that disturbs me with the joy
Of elevated thoughts; a sense sublime
Of something far more deeply infused,
Whose dwelling is the light of setting suns,
And the round ocean and the living air,
And the blue sky, and in the mind of man;
A motion and a spirit, that impels
All thinking things, all objects of thought,
And rolls through all things.

WILLIAM WORDSWORTH, *Tintern Abbey*

INTRODUCTION

The relationship with my body intelligence is ongoing. In *Good Morning Henry*, we've focused on the reasons why we become ill and how to regain physical, emotional, mental and spiritual health. Illness usually results from erroneous beliefs and thoughts that lead to negative emotions that cause continual anxiety as well as dis-ease. We've examined how to restore balance and peace to ourselves and our world. In doing this, we discussed the importance of acknowledging—although that is too weak a word—the sentience of all life-forms on Earth, including animals, trees, plants, birds, fish and minerals. Our discussion broadened to include the evolution of the Earth and the universal consciousness that creates all life in our universe and how to work with nature to embrace the guardianship of the Earth that is humanity's destiny.

When I first began writing this book, I thought that it would be a self-help book containing exercises to work with the body intelligence, solely with the physical body. However, my body intelligence wanted to discuss the causes and not the symptoms of illness, so you could heal yourself at source. I agree with Henry that this is the most efficient, practical method to restore mental, emotional and, ultimately, physical health, as physical illness and disease are most often the result of erroneous thoughts and disconnection to the universal life force. Yet, having said that, I'm also aware that you, dear reader, may want more information about your physical body to assist you in the process of healing.

To that end, I have two recommendations.

1. Many of you will feel moved by what Henry has said and will want to develop a relationship with your body intelligence. Our mp3 *Healing with the Body Elemental* will help you to examine all organs in your body, look at erroneous thoughts and find solutions to maximize health in your life. See: https://www.myspiritualtransformation.com/audio/.

2. The second recommendation is to read the section 'Your Body Has a Message for You' and contemplate what your body may be trying to tell you.

19
YOUR BODY HAS
A MESSAGE FOR YOU

After reading my conversations with Henry, you may still have questions about specific illnesses and physical conditions. Over the years, I too have been seeking to understand how certain thoughts contribute to physical illness. In the following section, I want to share with you insights that I've found helpful from my own life and from working with others in healing workshops and in individual therapy sessions. This information is not given as a medical diagnosis, as I have no training in this area. However, as a psychotherapist, I've given workshops to psychiatrists, physicians and other health professionals, as well as the general public, in working with the body elemental, the body intelligence to determine the thoughts and feelings that cause your physical problems.

Nevertheless, I believe that you are your own best authority. I encourage you to use my suggestions as pointers and also tap into your inner intuition to find the answers. Furthermore, rather than thinking of your ailment as an enemy that must be overcome, consider it a friend that is giving you a valuable lesson and ask yourself, "What is the lesson?" Remember always to love and be grateful to your body for allowing you to enjoy this beautiful world. Continue to focus on the positive and celebrate what is working in your body instead of focusing solely on what is not working. This attitude is the path to wellness.

With this in mind, let's examine some possible thoughts and feelings that may cause difficulties in your body and how you might heal yourself. We'll examine the major organs and the ailments affecting them beginning with the head.

Physical Problems: Causes and Solutions

BRAIN

If you are having a problem with your brain, such as a **Brain Tumor**, could it be that you are unwilling to change the way you think about yourself and others? If this is the case, the solution may be to embrace the world as it is and others as they are. A **Concussion** may be caused by unwillingness to change an outmoded thought that needs to be released. Consider: What might that thought be? Replace that thought with a new one and move fearlessly into embracing life.

What if your problem is a **Stroke**? Ask yourself, "Is the message for me to slow down and either stop what I'm doing or change the direction I'm going?" Take time, a lot of time, for inner reflection and to contemplate this question. Are you being forced into a more dependent state to receive from others and to learn humility? What is the gift in this situation? Embrace the gift.

Are your **Migraine Headaches** possibly caused by giving yourself pressure to be perfect rather than to love yourself as you are? If so, the solution could be to love yourself more and let go of the need to prove yourself to others.

Epilepsy is most common in children; however it can begin throughout life. Its main cause may be not wanting to be alive because of fear that you cannot cope. Ask yourself, "Do I have this fear?" If so, the solution is to realize that you are alive for a reason and to trust that you have all the gifts and attributes needed to fulfill your purpose.

With **Parkinson's Disease**, the dopamine in the brain that gives pleasure and allows us to plan is reduced. The underlying cause can be a fear of losing control. Consider: "Is this my issue?" If so, the solution is deep surrender to universal consciousness and trusting that you are safe in its loving care.

What if your problem is **Senile Dementia or Alzheimer's Disease**? The cause may be a desire to leave this world. Is this necessarily a bad thing? Each of us has free will to choose to fully accept a physical ailment or to attempt to heal it. It's important not to judge another's choice as we are not in their shoes.

For example, my mother had senile dementia and people loved to be with her as she was so peaceful and good-humored. She was no longer curious about the world. Once, I suggested that we watch a television special and she replied, "I've already seen it." This was impossible and yet, in a deeper way, she meant she had already seen everything that the illusionary world could present. These repetitive patterns no longer attracted her.

If, however, you genuinely want to stay in a physical body, then the solution is different. Find something to live for, or to which you can contribute, and do that. If the disease progresses even when you are doing this, understand that the veil between the physical and astral worlds is thinning so that you can move with more ease into the astral world. This is a gift as we all go to the astral realm when we die and this is a less difficult way to proceed than some others.

EYES

We know that it takes one-fifth of a second for what we see visually to travel along optic nerves and into the brain to be processed and understood. This means we don't actually live in the present but in the past. There is a time-lag. This time-lag is a gift that creates a built-in pause for us to witness our thoughts, change our interpretation of what we see happening and perceive the situation in a new way unclouded by old habits, wounds and programs.

The **cornea** of your eye does two-thirds of the focusing. If you are having difficulties with your cornea, ask yourself if you are focusing on the wrong things at this time in your life? Once you discover what this is, you might want to change your focus.

Glaucoma is caused by increased pressure on the optic nerve of your eye and **Macular Degeneration** is caused by increased pressure on the retina. So, ask yourself the questions, "What pressures are in my life currently?" and "How do I reduce or eliminate them?" "Am I causing my own pressures by being a perfectionist, clinging to an old way of being or a hurt suffered in the past?" These are only ideas to start you asking your own questions. Once you determine what pressures you are giving yourself, the solution often lies within your power to eliminate them. It may involve you forgiving someone or changing something in your life that you see as causing the problem.

The most common occurrence for eye problems as we age is **Cataracts**. Doctors believe this can be caused by oxidative stress that damages fats and proteins in the lens of the eye causing the lens to become cloudy. Studies have shown that increasing your intake of fruits and vegetables is helpful to prevent and/or delay the onset of cataracts. In addition, you might want to stay flexible by doing things differently and welcoming the future instead of fearing it. Cataract surgery is a simple procedure to restore your sight. It's important not to reject surgery as a solution to some physical problems. However, consider surgery as one option after identifying the underlying cause of your problem and correcting any erroneous thoughts that may have caused it.

EARS

The medical causes of most hearing problems are not known. For example, **Meniere's Disease** and **Labyrinthitis**, with symptoms of vertigo, nausea and ringing in the ears, may be caused by viruses, autoimmune reactions, genetic and environmental factors. These conditions are usually accompanied by inflammation and increased pressure in the fluid of the inner ear. The underlying cause of these problems may be not listening to what the universe is asking of you currently. Ask yourself, "Am I stubborn in wanting to do things my way?" "Am I unwilling to change?" If so, trust universal consciousness and surrender to what it wants of you. You may be feeling that you are going to lose something by doing this, but you will grow by listening and following its guidance.

Do you have **Tinnitus** or are you becoming hard of hearing? If you are having problems hearing what others say, ask yourself, "Am I open to other people's thoughts and beliefs, or do I wish to cling to mine?" Even if you don't agree with the other person's point of view, you can still be a sympathetic listener without changing your beliefs. Ultimately, the question is, "Am I open to listening to deeper truths from Spirit?"

TEETH, TONGUE, THROAT

The simplest way to discover the cause of problems with any organ is to examine its location in the body and its main function. Doing this with the mouth and throat, your immediate thought is that teeth chew your food and the tongue tastes your food, giving you sensory pleasure or displeasure. With this in mind, let's examine the causes and solutions of difficulties with the teeth and tongue.

Edgar Cayce, the renowned medium, once said that **Losing Teeth** can be related to losing your values or money. Louise Hay, author of *Heal Your Body*, says that it has to do with longstanding indecisiveness. I agree with both of these points of view as chewing on a problem for too long leads to procrastination. This may stem from fear of making a mistake. Examine your options and ask yourself, "Realistically, what are the worst and best things that could happen?" A positive solution is to examine your options, make a decision and act.

The tongue and larynx are needed to speak and if you are having problems with these organs, such as **Tongue, Throat or Laryngeal Cancer**, ask yourself, "Are my words kind while still being truthful?" "What would be best to say in what situation and what would be best not to say?" "Am I too critical?" Your answers to these questions might indicate what to change in order to heal. The tongue also gives us pleasure in tasting all that the world and life have to offer. So, find joy in life and speak in a positive way with love and kindness.

Tonsillitis and **Laryngitis** often represent the fear of speaking up and repressed anger. If this is your issue, the solution is to do what you fear.

HEART

Heart Disease is currently the Western world's leading cause of death killing the same number of Americans as the combined total for cancer, influenza, pneumonia and accidents. A century earlier, at a time when people didn't live long enough to suffer from diseased hearts, heart disease would have had stiff competition from infectious diseases such as typhoid and tuberculosis. Earlier in this book, we discussed the thoughts and emotions that contribute to a healthy heart. The only pointer I want to reinforce here is that the heart is not just a physical organ pumping blood, it's also a sensitive organ that responds to feelings.

If you have health issues stemming from the heart and cardiovascular system, such as **Arteriosclerosis, Heart Attacks**, or **Hypertension**, ask yourself, "Am I too sensitive to whether or not others like me?" "Have I hardened my heart to someone, or to many people?" "Do I put money or possessions ahead of love?" "Am I too emotional, taking situations too personally?" These questions may seem contradictory; however, each of these situations may cause heart problems. The solution, as we have said previously, is to do the opposite of what you've been doing. For example, if you are hardening your heart to someone, practice forgiveness. And if you are overly sensitive to others, develop self-love—and don't look outside yourself for this. Consider what acts of love your heart needs from you.

BLOOD

Henry said that the body intelligence travels in the blood throughout the body. The blood is the messenger service of the body keeping all parts of the body in communication and harmony. We know scientifically that red blood cells carry oxygen, hormones and vital chemicals to our cells and that white blood cells, as one of the body's defense systems, kill pathogens. Although scientists have been attempting for over 50 years to create artificial blood, they've been unsuccessful until now. Blood is a living substance that deteriorates outside the body. Doctors have discovered that it's usually better to allow a patient to replace their own blood—even if that involves them becoming anemic—than to give them someone else's blood especially if it's more than a few weeks old. Why? Because our blood is unique to us.

Some blood diseases, such as **Anemia**, result in decreased hemoglobin that leads to fatigue. Ask yourself, "Do I feel unloved or lack joy?" If so, these feelings may cause anemia. The solution could be to do what you love and associate with people who give you love. You might also benefit from building your self-love. **Recurring Infections** reveal that the white blood cells are not functioning well. This can be caused by not having boundaries. One solution is to stand up for yourself.

Hemophilia, which is the inability of the blood to clot, may be caused by giving too much and not knowing your limits. Assess what you can reasonably do and do only that.

Leukemia, cancer of the blood, starts in the bone marrow and produces abnormal blood cells. As with any cancer, ask yourself, "Am I resisting doing what my higher self wants?" "Am I feeling helpless and despondent?" If you discover an area where you believe this is the case, change that immediately. Ultimately, universal consciousness is self-love, love of others and love of all life. The solution to most physical problems lies in embodying some message of love.

LUNGS

In addition to helping the heart move oxygen-rich blood around the body, the lungs are very effective at removing pollutants and irritants of all kinds by coughing, sneezing or allowing irritants to be coughed up and swallowed so they'll be dissolved by stomach acids.

Pneumonia is an inflammation of the lungs caused by fatigue, giving up the will to live, or a rundown state caused by other illnesses. A solution is to use positive thinking and ask yourself, "What do I want to do now and in my life?" Then, set clear goals that give you joy and a reason to recover.

One of the most common illnesses is **Lung Cancer**. According to various studies, smokers are between 30 and 50 times more likely to get lung cancer than non-smokers. An obvious solution would be for smokers to give up smoking. If you are a smoker, ask yourself, "Why do I smoke?" "Am I pushing down something that is too uncomfortable to think or feel?" Perhaps you are afraid to say what you really feel for fear of rejection, or maybe you feel unloved. The solution then is to say what you wish and ask for what you want.

Most often, **Asthma** begins in children and 75 percent of children outgrow it as adults. The causes and cures for asthma are still hotly debated in medical circles and range from neurological factors to allergies. The possible underlying cause is an inclusion issue: Do you feel unsafe, unloved, or that you don't fit in? When you are afraid, you likely don't breathe deeply.

Thus, the solution is not to be overly sensitive to others' reactions to you and to become your own person, knowing that you are safe and loved by the universe.

LIVER

Glands are organs that secrete chemicals. Our largest internal gland is the liver. It has many functions, including secreting bile to digest our food, filtering toxins, absorbing vitamins, converting glucose and eliminating red blood cells at the end of their life. We can regrow two-thirds of our liver if it is damaged but, without it, we die.

In alchemy, the liver is associated with both melancholy and choler, sadness and anger. In our modern world, many individuals feel disempowered and helpless to take control of their lives. These feelings negatively affect the liver. The most common liver disease is **Fatty Liver** which is caused by too much fat in liver cells. Often, we don't know we have it until it's too late. Fatty liver disease is on the increase and now is even affecting children. It's caused mostly by our modern diet. Physical solutions are: Don't eat processed foods. Instead, focus on eating fresh fruits and vegetables to detoxify yourselves to clean your liver. Drink large amounts of pure water and, lastly, get lots of exercise and sun.

The long-term solution is to choose to do something within your sphere of influence, using your particular interests and gifts. For example, meditate daily on peace and a healthy Earth. Canvass for a political candidate who stands for your values. Clean up trash weekly in your local park. Choose something, then act and stay optimistic, trusting in the universe's plan for you and our world.

Alcoholism, which can cause **Cirrhosis** of the liver, may be caused by wanting to numb and kill pain of feeling separate. This separation may have originated from feeling unloved as a child—a feeling which you have brought into adult life. However, ultimately, it's the illness of separation from universal consciousness. Ask yourself, "Is this true of me?" The solution has already been mentioned: value yourself, increase your self-love and know you have nothing to give or do in order to be loved.

GALLBLADDER

The gallbladder is an organ that we can live without as shown by thousands of individuals who do just this. However, universal intelligence makes no mistakes in the organs it gives us. All have a purpose and it's important to ask yourself what that is. It's also preferable to keep the original body parts if it's possible to adequately repair them. If it's not possible, send your body love and gratitude prior to and after your surgery and realize that your organ still exists etherically.

The gallbladder stores the bile produced by the liver and secretes it into the intestines. Occasionally, these ducts are blocked by gallstones. Having a lot of gall metaphorically has come to mean that a person is pushy and aggressive. **Gallstones** may arise if you have hardened yourself to something. If you have gallstones, ask yourself: "Have I become too inflexible or opinionated?" "Am I clinging to the past?" If so, stop pushing down your frustration. Go with the flow of life, and start moving again by exercising more and sitting less.

PANCREAS

The pancreas is a gland that we need for life. It produces some digestive enzymes as well as the hormone insulin that regulates blood sugars.

The incidence of **Diabetes**, probably the most well-known disease affecting the pancreas, is increasing dramatically. One possibility is that people are adopting a poor diet and not exercising or walking enough. Additionally, diabetes is associated with disappointment, sadness and feeling unloved either by others or by life in general. You could ask yourself, "Do I feel that I deserve more happiness than what I have?" and "Do I attempt to give myself the sweetness that others or life is not giving me?" If so, the solution may be gratitude for all that you have rather than feeling you have less than others.

Pancreatitis has a similar cause: that your life is disappointing. If so, find joy in all that you have been given in life and let your energy flow into your new attitude with joy.

SPLEEN

The spleen filters our blood by recycling old red blood cells and storing white blood cells to fight infections and strengthen our immune system. Luckily, we can live without a spleen, but do we really want to?

If you have **Inflammation of the Spleen**, which can happen with **Lupus, Rheumatoid Arthritis**, and **Mononucleosis**, do you feel unsafe? Ask yourself, "What am I fighting?" "What or who is the enemy?" The solution may be to increase your faith in universal consciousness and trust that you are loved and taken care of.

KIDNEYS

As with diabetes, the incidence of kidney disease is rising. Kidneys filter wastes and regulate the chemistry of the blood, especially salt.

Similar to the gallbladder, the kidneys may develop **Kidney Stones** that can cause pain and need to be removed. Why? Eating processed foods, so prevalent in our modern world, causes many of our health problems. Antioxidant foods, such as berries, cabbage, onions and garlic, strengthen the kidneys and are good to add to your diet. Also, let's examine possible erroneous thoughts and solutions to kidney problems.

If you store negativity in your life—either towards yourself, others, or life in general—you may develop **Kidney Disease**. Kidneys are organs of elimination, so ask yourself, "What negative feelings am I not eliminating?" Try letting go of needing to have things your way and let go of the past and live in the present.

ADRENAL GLANDS

The adrenal glands, located on top of the kidneys, excrete hormones to help regulate stress, the immune system, metabolism and blood pressure. We cannot live without our adrenal glands. It's common for individuals to suffer from **Adrenal Fatigue**—a disease due to the stress of our modern world.

Tiredness, weakness and having difficulty sleeping can be symptoms of **Adrenal Fatigue**, as can craving salt, sugar and caffeine. The causes may be overwork or a great deal of stress over a long period. These can lead to depression and other serious illnesses. Ask yourself, "Am I being overly responsible and caring for others more than I care for myself?" "Am I not enjoying life and what I'm doing?" If this is the case, the solution is to care for yourself and do what gives you joy.

Less common diseases of the adrenals are **Cushing Syndrome** resulting from too much cortisol and **Addison's Disease** resulting from too little. Both can be treated by replacing the missing hormones, however the underlying causes and solutions are the same as for adrenal fatigue.

BLADDER

The kidneys eliminate toxins through the bladder as urine. The bladder can have stones that may need to be eliminated through surgery.

As with the kidneys, bladder problems can be caused by not eliminating thoughts and feelings that you need to release. This stems from a fear of losing control which can result in **Bladder Stones** or **Incontinence**, a condition that forces you to confront loss of control.

Bladder Cancer is much more common in smokers than non-smokers, so eliminating smoking not only helps to prevent lung cancer, it can also help prevent bladder cancer. Physically, to prevent or help cure **Bladder Infections** or **Bladder Cancer**, it's good to drink lots of water to help with elimination, accompanied by the thought, "This is the water of life and I'm purifying myself for the next step in my life's journey." Bladder problems may indicate that you have stored anger from the past of which you may not be conscious. It's time to let go of all anger and resentment and enjoy what life offers.

STOMACH, INTESTINES AND COLON

The stomach excretes hydrochloric acid to help digest our food. The acid also kills a lot of bacteria in food that otherwise might make us ill. Most of the actual digestion happens in the small and, to some extent, large intestines (also called the colon). The small intestine does 90 percent of the digestion and absorption of vitamins and minerals in food, and the colon completes the process for hard-to-digest materials and extracts water to give back to the body.

Stomach or Small Intestinal Ulcers—according to medical sources—are often caused by bacteria or long-term use of ASA or ibuprofen. However, one of the underlying physical causes can be a poor diet that doesn't include vegetables, especially cruciferous vegetables like cabbage and broccoli. A deeper cause is the inability to digest what is happening in your life, leaving you fearful or angry. If so, the solution may be to examine what you are afraid of. Ask yourself: "Am I afraid of the future?" or "Is there something in the present that I cannot accept?" Deep surrender and acceptance of whatever you fear will help you overcome this physical problem.

Appendicitis and **Crohn's Disease** affect the far end of the small intestine. **Celiac Disease** also affects the small intestine. Both Crohn's disease and celiac disease are increasing at an alarming rate. They are autoimmune diseases caused by inflammation which results in the body attacking itself. As with ulcers, ask yourself, "What can't I accept?" "Am I a perfectionist who feels that I can never get things right?" "Do I feel like I've lost control of my life?" Diseases linked to excretion carry some stigma, so you may have an issue with shame or guilt. You might also be holding resentment. Examine these possible causes and practice self-love and letting go of these feelings, so that you can move on with your life.

The colon is the seat of many diseases including **Irritable Bowel Syndrome, Colitis, Constipation** and **Bowel Cancer.** Eating more fiber and exercise are healthy things to do for bowel health, however the underlying causes and solutions that we have already mentioned will help to remedy these situations.

UTERUS, OVARIES, BREASTS FOR WOMEN
PENIS, TESTES, PROSTATE FOR MEN

Endometriosis and **Uterine Fibroids** may be caused by wanting to grow something but in an inappropriate way. For a woman suffering from these, ask yourself, "What do I really want to create?" Find a way to do this in a healthy way.

Ovarian Cancer and **Cervical Cancer** can stem from ambivalent feelings about womanhood, fear of aging and concern over what you can still birth into the world. Cervical cancer is 70 percent more common in women who have had **Vaginal Warts**, which may, in turn, be caused by ambivalent feelings and shame about sex. The solution could be to flood your body with joy and enjoyment in appreciating womanhood in all ways and ages. Focus on what you want to do that gives you joy.

Breast Cancer can indicate issues with your mother or ambivalence about being a woman and resentment about nurturing others. The solutions are to explore your own creativity and nurture yourself with what gives you joy.

Sexually transmitted diseases have underlying causes of shame, dishonoring of yourself and needing to be punished. The cure may lie in deep forgiveness for choices you have made in the past, and love and acceptance of yourself. Feel yourself empowered and vital.

Erectile Dysfunction can be caused by ambivalent feelings about sex related to shame and/or fears of aging and losing your masculinity, and possibly issues with a parent. These masculine issues may also be related to **Prostate and Testicular Cancer** which have similar causes. If so, the solution is to love every aspect of your body, including your sexual organs and their function. Think of yourself as powerful and accomplishing your goals in life.

BONES, BACK AND JOINTS

Approximately half of American women and one in four men are likely to break bones as they age which, in turn, can lead to never fully recovering. Bones are alive and grow stronger through exercise, so it's essential to exercise. According to current statistics, going for regular walks also reduces risk of heart attack and stroke by 31 percent. Walking also helps to prevent and cure obesity which is skyrocketing in middle-and higher-income countries. Let's now look at underlying causes of bone, back and joint problems.

Being overweight and a lack of exercise are known to cause back and joint problems but there are other causes as well. **Obesity** often results from over-eating and/or eating the 'wrong' foods which are fat, starchy or sweet, as found in pre-packaged, fast foods. The underlying cause may be wanting easy fulfillment due to low self-esteem and fear of failure. These relate to self-condemnation. Consider: "Are these examples true for you?" If so, the solution is to set a goal and get support for sticking to it. This will increase self-esteem and a sense of success. As your health improves, you will have more energy to accomplish more goals and more years in which to do it.

Another cause of **Back Problems, Sciatica** or **Broken Bones** could be that you are holding yourself back from doing something. Ask yourself, "Do I believe I can achieve my goals?" "Would I like someone to look after me?" "Do I need a rest because I've been doing too much?" "Am I supported by others?" The solution is to take time to pause in a positive way, not by being resentful or frustrated. Rest and contemplate what would make you happy, then commit to that goal and start.

Causes of **Osteoarthritis** and **Rheumatoid Arthritis** may include feeling resentful that you are doing too much, as in: "See how much I do!" or "Why doesn't anyone ever help me?" The feeling can be self-critical— that you aren't doing enough—or being critical of others that they aren't doing more. Solutions that might help are to accept and love yourself and others unconditionally, and be grateful for all you have and for others in your life without having to change anything. All is perfect as it is.

SKIN AND ALLERGIES

The skin is our largest organ and it physically separates us from others. If you have skin problems such as **Eczema, Psoriasis**, or **Boils**, something in you may be wanting to come out. Consider: "Am I angry or afraid of others?" "Do I feel unloved and unlovable?" The solutions to these negative thoughts are self-love, self-care and reducing perfect standards for yourself and others.

Allergies may affect the skin but they can attack any organ. If they produce a life-threatening reaction, then of course it's best to avoid the trigger. However, if you find your skin is reacting to an increasing number of triggers, reflect on the pointers mentioned above, and ask yourself, "What am I allergic to in life?" The solutions are to embrace life whole-heartedly and find joy in everything rather than to be negative, complaining and self-denying of joy.

CONCLUSION

As you observe, the causes of most physical problems are feeling guilty, resentful, angry or helpless. Underlying these negative emotions is usually a deeper cause related to love. When in doubt about how to heal yourself, the solution is most often UNCONDITIONAL self-love, along with love of others and love of your life.

SIGNS OF SPIRITUAL TRANSFORMATION

Discover if you are going through a spiritual transformation by completing a few quick and easy questions.

☐ Yes ☐ No	1. Are you going through deep questioning about what you are doing in some aspect of your life?
☐ Yes ☐ No	2. Do you feel overwhelmed?
☐ Yes ☐ No	3. Are you having more difficulty controlling your emotions and do you cry or become angry more often?
☐ Yes ☐ No	4. Do you feel that you can no longer do the same things or be the same person as before and yet are not sure what steps to take to change?
☐ Yes ☐ No	5. Do your old roles of parent, partner, friend or co-worker no longer serve you and are you wanting to change your relationships?
☐ Yes ☐ No	6. Do you feel like you are only living a fraction of who you are and do you want to fully embrace your whole self?
☐ Yes ☐ No	7. Do you experience floating anxiety and worry and increasingly want to find peace and happiness?
☐ Yes ☐ No	8. Are you tired of quick fixes such as buying a new car, house, holiday etc. that give only fleeting happiness? Are you now wanting to find long-lasting peace?

☐ Yes ☐ No	9. Do you feel out of control?
☐ Yes ☐ No	10. Do others seem no longer comfortable with you? Are they reacting to you differently and/or are friendships and relationships ending?
☐ Yes ☐ No	11. Do you feel your life has moved into unknown territory where you no longer know the rules?
☐ Yes ☐ No	12. Are you questioning values that you have held dear for most of your life?
☐ Yes ☐ No	13. Are you interested in spiritual topics and in developing your spiritual gifts to become your authentic self?

If, in addition to the previous questions, you also agree with the following ones, the intensity of your signs of spiritual transformation increase:

☐ Yes ☐ No	14. Have you suffered a major setback in your life such as a health crisis, death of a loved one, relationship ending or career setback?
☐ Yes ☐ No	15. Are you feeling spiritually lost?

If the majority of your answers to these questions are '**YES**', you are going through a spiritual transformation. Although you might feel overwhelmed and are experiencing inner and outer stress with what appears to be a negative time in your life, in fact this transformation is positive. You have learned and grown as much as you could up until now with your ego/personality in charge. Now your soul is calling you to become the REAL authentic you.

For a **FREE Spiritual Transformation Kit**
https://www.myspiritualtransformation.com/start-for-free/

For information, exercises and solutions to assist you
https://www.myspiritualtransformation.com

ADDITIONAL RESOURCES TO HELP YOU

✳ We offer courses in *Self-Healing with the Body Intelligence* to assist you to work more deeply with your body intelligence on the various issues discussed in this book. Our courses include workbooks with various mp3s for self or group study and are available at **https://myspiritualtransformation.com**

✳ To work more deeply on overcoming your fears in *Chapter 4: Do Fears Jerk your Leash*, I recommend our *Fear Transformed* self-study course. It includes a 70-page workbook with 4 mp3s and 2 videos and is available at: **https://myspiritualtransformation.com/product/fear-transformed-self-study**

✳ To clear your etheric body of negative thoughtforms as discussed in *Chapter 6: Negative Beliefs…Begone!* and *Chapter 8: You are a Hologram*, I recommend the *Transform Yourself* self-study course, which includes a 70-page workbook and 4 etheric clearing mp3s to clear your central channel and eliminate negative thoughtforms. It is available at: **https://myspiritualtransformation.com/product/transform-yourself-self-study**

✳ To examine your family's and ancestors' life scripts in more detail, as discussed in *Chapter 5: Free Yourself from Inherited Life Scripts*, I recommend our *Ancestor and Family Healing* self-study course which includes a comprehensive workbook with many exercises and 9 mp3s/videos. It is available at: **https://www.myspiritualtransformation.com/shop-courses**

✳ More information on the spiritual evolution of animals, birds, fish, trees, plants and minerals discussed in *Chapter 16: Discover the Consciousness of Animals, Birds and Fish* and *Chapter 17: Discover The Consciousness of Trees, Plants and Minerals* is found in *Decoding Your Destiny* by Tanis Helliwell.

✳ More information on elementals and other life-forms evolving on Earth and other planets, which is discussed in *Chapter 18: We We We All the Way Home*, is found in Tanis Helliwell's books *Decoding Your Destiny*, *Summer with the Leprechauns*, *Pilgrimage with the Leprechauns*, *High Beings of Hawaii* and *Hybrids: So you think you are human.*

ACKNOWLEDGEMENTS

This book would not have been possible if not for the considerable time and effort that Simon Goede devoted to helping me clarify murky points, encouraging me to give examples to illustrate what I was ineptly trying to explain. I'm grateful for his patience as we edited again and again.

Donna Miniely came to the rescue lifting the work to higher heights of clarity and with a kind touch through our many discussions and editing. Thanks also to Merle Dulmadge who built on these suggestions.

I am grateful to Patrick Crean for his kind encouragement in turning the rather cerebral draft into a user-friendly book that others could put into practice in their lives. I liken him to a master chef who keeps tasting the dish and applying the right spice until you want to eat your own dish.

Also, I want to acknowledge Stephen Roberts who, with his deep anthroposophical knowledge, helped me illuminate points that many would have found overly complex. Finally, when it was time for what I hoped was the last edit Janet Rouss, Jenny Lou Linley and Connie Phenix dove in with their creative and patient word-smithing.

The cover and book layout is designed by Melany Hallam. Thank you so much for your beautiful creation.

Lastly, thanks to my eagle-eyed friend Monika Bernegg who proofreads all my work and finds 'peanuts' even after my twelfth edit.

BOOKS YOU MIGHT FIND HELPFUL

Although this is not a bibliography as such, many books have influenced me over the years. I include some of these from Eastern and Western spiritual traditions, as well as those with a more scientific bent.

FOR CHAPTERS ON THE IMPORTANCE OF THE BRAIN, HEART AND NEW SCIENCE

Rudolph Ballentine, MD., *Radical Healing*, Three Rivers Press, New York, 1999.

Gregg Braden, *The Science of Self-Empowerment: Awakening the New Human Story*, Hay House, 2019.

Bill Bryson, *The Body*, Doubleday Canada, 2019.

Dana Cohen and Gina Bria, *Quench*, Hachette Books, NY, 2018.

Joe Dispenza, *Becoming Supernatural: How common people are doing the uncommon*, Hay House, 2019.

Norman Doidge, MD., *The Brain That Changes Itself*, Penguin Books, 2007.

Louise Hay, *Heal your Body*, Hay House, CA, 1994.

Robert Lanza, MD., *Biocentrism: How Life and Consciousness are the Keys to Understanding the True Nature of the Universe*, BenBella Books, Dallas, TX, 2010.

Sayer Ji, *Regenerate*, Hay House Inc., NY, 2020.

Bruce Lipton, *The Biology of Belief*, Hay House Inc., CA, 2015.

Rollin McCraty, Mike Atkinson, Dana Tomasino, Raymond Trevor Bradley, *The Coherent Heart*, Institute of HeartMath, 2006.

Lynn McTaggart, *The Field*, Harper Perennial, 2008.

Andrew Newberg, *How God Changes Your Brain*, Ballantine Books, New York, 2010.

Christiane Northrup, *Making Life Easy: How the Divine Inside can Heal your Body and your Life*, Hay House, 2018.

Alberto Villoldo, *One Spirit Medicine*, Hay House Inc., CA, 2015.

Anthony William, *Medical Medium*, Hay House Inc., CA, 2015.

FOR CHAPTERS ON THE CONSCIOUSNESS OF ANIMALS, TREES, PLANTS

Temple Grandin and Catherine Johnson, *Animals in Translation*, Schreibner, New York, 2006.

Tanis Helliwell, *Summer with the Leprechauns*, Wayshower Enterprises, BC, 1997 and 2011.

Jeffrey Masson and Susan McCarthy, *When Elephants Weep: The emotional lives of animals*, Delta Book, New York, 1995.

Rupert Sheldrake, *Dogs that know when their owners are coming home,* Three Rivers Press, New York, 2011.

David Suzuki, *The Sacred Balance*, Greystone Books, Vancouver, BC, 1997.

Peter Tompkins and Christopher Bird, *The Secret Life of Plants,* Harper & Row, NY, 1973.

Peter Wohlleben, *The Inner Life of Animals*, Greystone Books, Vancouver, BC, 2017.

Peter Wohlleben, *The Hidden Life of Trees*, Greystone Books, Vancouver, BC, 2016.

FOR CHAPTERS ON MINDFULNESS AND CONSCIOUSNESS

Ram Dass, *Paths to God: Living the Bhagavad-Gita,* Three Rivers Press, New York, 2004.

Matthew Fox, *Original Blessing*, Jeremy Tarcher, New York, 2000.

Gangaji, *The Diamond in Your Pocket*, Sounds True, Boulder, CO, 2005.

David Hawkins, *The Eye of the I*, Veritas Publishing, Sedona, AZ, 2001.

David Hawkins, *I: Reality and Subjectivity*, Veritas Publishing, Sedona, AZ, 2003.

David Hawkins, *Transcending the Levels of Consciousness*, Veritas Publishing, Sedona, AZ, 2006.

Tanis Helliwell, *Decoding Your Destiny*, Wayshower Enterprises, Vancouver, BC, 2011.

Tanis Helliwell, *Manifest Your Soul's Purpose*, Wayshower Enterprises, Vancouver, BC, 2012.

Jean Houston, *The Wizard of Us*, Atria, New York, 2012.

Catherine Ingram, *Passionate Presence*, Gotham Books, New York, 2003.

Gopi Krishna, *Kundalini: The Evolutionary Energy in Man*, Shambhala, Boston, 1997.

Jack Kornfield and Joseph Goldstein, *Seeking the Heart of Wisdom*, Shambhala, Boston, 1987.

Jack Kornfield, *A Path with Heart*, Bantam Books, New York, 1993.

Gerald G. May, *The Dark Night of the Soul*, HarperOne, New York, 2004.

Juan Mascaro, translator of *The Bhagavad-Gita*, Penguin Books, New York, 1962.

Franklin Merrell-Wolff, *Pathways Through to Space: A personal report of transformation in consciousness*, The Julian Press, New York, 1973.

Patanjali, *How to Know God: The Yoga Aphorisms of Patanjali*, translated by Swami Prabhavananda and Christopher Isherwood, Vedanta Press, CA, 1953.

Prajnaparamita, *Wings of Freedom*, Dharma Chakra Publications, The Netherlands, 2019.

Michael Roads, *From Illusion to Enlightenment*, Six Degrees Publishing Group, Portland, OR, 2017.

Richard Rudd, *Gene Keys*, Watkins, London, UK, 2013.

Michael Singer, *The Untethered Soul*, New Harbinger Publications, Oakland, CA, 2007.

Michael Singer, *The Surrender Experiment*, Harmony, New York, 2015.

Sri Aurobindo, *A Greater Psychology*, Jeremy Tarcher, New York, 2001.

Rudolf Steiner, *How to Know Higher Worlds*, Anthroposophic Press, Great Barrington, MA, 2002.

Rudolf Steiner, *Theosophy*, Anthroposophic Press, New York, 1994.

Eckhart Tolle, *The Power of Now*, New World Library, Novato, CA, 1998.

Eckhart Tolle, *A New Earth*, Dutton, NY, 2005.

Two Disciples, *The Rainbow Bridge*, the Triune Foundation, Escondido, CA, 1981.

Paramahansa Yogananda, *Autobiography of a Yogi*, Self-Realization Fellowship, Los Angeles, 1946.

Paramahansa Yogananda, *The Science of Religion*, Self-Realization Fellowship, Los Angeles, 1982.

Paramahansa Yogananda, *Man's Eternal Quest*, Self-Realization Fellowship, Los Angeles, 1975.

Paramahansa Yogananda, *The Divine Romance*, Self-Realization Fellowship, Los Angeles, 1986.

Paramahansa Yogananda, *Journey to Self-Realization*, Self-Realization Fellowship, Los Angeles, 1997.

Paramahansa Yogananda, *The Bhagavad-Gita*, Self-Realization Fellowship, Los Angeles, 1995.

Paramahansa Yogananda, *The Second Coming of Christ*, Self-Realization Fellowship, Los Angeles, 2004.

AUDIO MP3S

Tanis Helliwell, *The Body Elemental*, https://www.myspiritualtransformation.com/audio/

Tanis Helliwell, *Rise of the Unconscious*, https://www.myspiritualtransformation.com/audio/

Tanis Helliwell, *Eliminating Negativity*, https://www. myspiritualtransformation.com/audio/

VIDEOS ON AMAZON PRIME VIDEO

Tanis Helliwell, *Spiritual Transformation*, **https://www.amazon.com/dp/B0069WJI88/**

Tanis Helliwell, *Elementals and Nature Spirits*, **https://www.amazon.com/dp/B01B6O1YLM/**

Tanis Helliwell, *Hybrids: So you think you are human*, **https://www.amazon.com/dp/B01AVB30SG/**

ABOUT THE AUTHOR

Tanis Helliwell has given transformation and healing workshops internationally for over 30 years. She is a leading-edge psychotherapist, well-known for working to heal physical, emotional and mental traumas and patterns. Tanis teaches her techniques internationally to groups of psychiatrists, physicians, psychotherapists as well as to the general public.

In addition to her psychotherapy practice and workshops, she worked consecutively for 30 years as a consultant to businesses, universities and government to create healthy organizations, and to help people develop their personal and professional potential. She was a faculty member of the Banff Centre for Leadership for over 20 years and numbered IBM, and many medical, social service and environmental agencies among her clients.

Tanis Helliwell is a sought-after keynote speaker whose insightful awareness is applied in a variety of disciplines. She has presented at conferences also featuring Rupert Sheldrake, Bruce Lipton, Matthew Fox, Barbara Marx Hubbard, Gregg Braden, Fritjof Capra, and Jean Houston. These conferences include The Science and Consciousness Conference in Albuquerque, The World Future Society in Washington, DC and Spirituality in Business conferences in Boston, Toronto, Vancouver and Mexico. She's also presented at Findhorn, Hollyhock, A.R.E. Edgar Cayce, Alice Bailey and Anthroposophical events.

In 2000, she founded the International Institute for Transformation (IIT) which offers programs to assist individuals to become conscious creators to work with the spiritual laws that govern our world. Tanis teaches annually in The UK, The Netherlands, Germany, Switzerland, US and Canada as well as Sweden, France and others. Since 2020, when travel became difficult, she has been offering LIVE Online courses in topics such as Transform Yourself, Co-creating with Nature Spirits to Heal the Earth and Ancestor and Family Healing.

She is the author of the classic *Summer with the Leprechauns* as well as *Pilgrimage with the Leprechauns, Take Your Soul to Work, Manifest Your Soul's Purpose, Decoding Your Destiny, Hybrids* and *The High Beings of Hawaii: Encounters with mystical ancestors*. Her books have been translated into 7 different languages.

She is committed to helping individuals to develop right relationships with themselves, others and the Earth.

TANIS HELLIWELL
1766 Hollingsworth Rd.,
Powell River, BC Canada V8A 0M4
tanis@tanishelliwell.com | tanishelliwell.com | facebook.com/Tanis.Helliwell

BOOKS BY TANIS HELLIWELL:

- High Beings of Hawaii: Encounters with mystical ancestors
- Hybrids: So you think you are human
- Summer with the Leprechauns: a true story
- Pilgrimage with the Leprechauns: a true story of a mystical tour of Ireland
- Decoding Your Destiny: keys to humanity's spiritual transformation
- Manifest Your Soul's Purpose
- Embraced by Love

VIDEOS ON AMAZON PRIME VIDEO

1. Elementals and Nature Spirits,
   https://www.amazon.com/dp/B01B6O1YLM/
2. Hybrids: So you think you are human,
   https://www.amazon.com/dp/B01AVB30SG/
3. Spiritual Transformation: Journey of Co-creation,
   https://www.amazon.com/dp/B0069WJI88/

MP3S AVAILABLE ON OUR WEBSITE

https://www.myspiritualtransformation.com

Series A – The Self-Healing Series: Talk and Visualization
1. The Body Elemental / Healing with the Body Elemental
2. Rise of the Unconscious / Your Basic Goodness
3. Reawakening Ancestral Memory / Through the Veil Between the Worlds

Series B – Spiritual Transformation Collection: Talk and Visualization
1. The Celtic Mysteries / Quest for the Holy Grail
2. The Egyptian Mysteries / Initiation in the Pyramid of Giza
3. The Greek Mysteries / Your Male and Female Archetypes
4. The Christian Mysteries / Jesus' Life: A Story of Initiation
5. Address from The Earth/ Manifesting Peace on Earth

Series C – Personal Growth Collection: Two Visualizations
1. Path of Your Life / Your Favorite Place
2. Eliminating Negativity / Purpose of Your Life
3. Linking Up World Servers / Healing the Earth

CPSIA information can be obtained
at www.ICGtesting.com
Printed in the USA
BVHW040839190422
634696BV00013B/193

9 781987 831320